Jer. Taylor

THE LIFE

OF

JEREMY TAYLOR,

BISHOP OF DOWN, CONNOR,
AND DROMORE.

BY

GEORGE L. DUYCKINCK.

NEW YORK:

General Protestant Episcopal Sunday School Union,
and Church Book Society,
762 BROADWAY.
1860.

PUBLISHED

BY THE SUNDAY SCHOOL CHILDREN

OF

ST. PAUL'S CHURCH, ALBANY,

New York.

THIS VOLUME IS DEDICATED TO

THE REV. FRANCIS L. HAWKS, D.D., LL.D.,

AS A RESPECTFUL AND GRATEFUL TRIBUTE

TO SERVICES

IN THE PULPIT, THE SCHOOLHOUSE, AND THE STUDY,

KINDRED WITH THOSE RECORDED

IN ITS PAGES.

PREFACE.

Owing to the unfortunate destruction by fire, early in the present century, of the papers illustrative of the career of Bishop Taylor, which had been collected from various branches of his family by his descendant, William Todd Jones, the original materials for the biography of the great divine are but scant. The few letters, however, which remain are sufficient to confirm the impression made upon us by his books.

We find Bishop Taylor at once earnest and genial; accepting privation and imprisonment rather than abate a jot of devotion to political principles believed essential to the welfare of Church and country, but bearing to the seclusion thus imposed a cheerful temper, and dividing his time between a provision, by the hard labor of the schoolmaster, for the temporal requirements of a large family, and a more bountiful endowment for the afflicted Church of his day and the larger family of his scattered brethren, which their descendants of more peaceful seasons have cherished and will ever cherish as among their choicest heritages.

The facts for the following pages have been derived from the funeral sermon by Dr. Rust, and the Lives of Bishop Taylor by Archdeacon Bonney, Bishop Heber, and the Rev. Mr. R. A. Willmott. The account of Rowland Taylor is drawn from the venerable Book of Martyrs. The passages from Bishop Taylor's writings have been selected with care in the endeavor to present, so far as a small volume would allow, the finest products of his glowing genius side by side with the incidents which in many cases gave them birth.

NEW YORK, *February* 10, 1860.

CONTENTS.

CHAPTER I.

CHAPTER II.

CHAPTER III.

CHAPTER IV.

PAGE

CHAPTER V.

CHAPTER VI.

CHAPTER VII.

CHAPTER VIII.

CHAPTER IX.

CHAPTER X.

CHAPTER XI.

CHAPTER XII.

CHAPTER XIII.

CHAPTER XIV.

CHAPTER XV.

CHAPTER XVI.

THE LIFE OF

JEREMY TAYLOR.

CHAPTER I.

HADLEY PARISH—DR. ROWLAND TAYLOR—INTRODUCTION OF THE MASS—STRUGGLE—DR. TAYLOR'S ARREST AND IMPRISONMENT—THE LITANY—INTERVIEW AT ST. BOTOLPH'S PORCH—LEAVING THE WOOLPACK INN—THOMAS TAYLOR AND JOHN HULL—CHEERFULNESS—"DEAR FATHER AND GOOD SHEPHERD"—PASSING THE ALMS-HOUSES—THE BLIND COUPLE—AT HOME—BRUTAL INSULTS—THE FIRE.

THE town of Hadley, in Suffolk, enjoys the honorable distinction of having been one of the first in all England to receive Protestantism. Under the direction of the worthy Dr. Thomas Bilney, the inhabitants became so versed in the Scriptures and theology, that "the whole town seemed rather a university of the learned than a town of cloth-making or laboring people."

Dr. Rowland Taylor came from the family

of Archbishop Cranmer to take charge of this well-prepared parish. He worked zealously as a rector, allowing no Sunday or Holyday, or other time when he could collect the people together, to pass without a sermon. His life and conversation were a perpetual exhortation to holiness by their display of its beauty. He was kind and charitable to the sick and needy, gentle to all; but when occasion of admonition arose, he spared neither rich nor poor. Love and favor naturally followed his footsteps as he walked through his parish, and this happy state of things continued all the days of King Edward's reign. The accession of Mary brought a terrible change, which Dr. Taylor was among the first to feel.

Roman Catholicism having been restored as the state worship, one Foster, "a certain petty gentleman after the sort of a lawyer," as he is oddly described by Fox, who adds, "a man of no great skill, but a bitter persecutor in those days," hired John Averth, the Romish parson of Aldam, "a very money mammonist," to come to Hadley church and celebrate mass therein. Preparations were commenced by setting up an altar, which was broken down. It was repaired, and a guard set to watch it.

The next day Foster appeared with one Clerke, of Hadley, and the Roman Catholic priest, and with armed retainers to prevent interference, commenced mass. Dr. Taylor, hearing the bells, repaired to the church; the doors were shut and barred, but passing to the rear he found the chancel door only latched. Entering, he at once denounced the proceedings, and commanded the "popish wolf" to begone. After a few words of discussion, the rector was forced out, and the mass continued. The people flocking to eject the abhorred worship, were refused admission. Some threw stones through the windows, narrowly missing the intruder.

A few days after, Dr. Taylor was ordered, on the complaint of Foster and Clerke, to appear before the Lord Chancellor, Stephen Gardiner, bishop of Winchester. His parishioners urged him to seek safety by flight. "Our Saviour Christ," they told him, "willeth and biddeth us that when they persecute us in one city we should fly to another." But Dr. Taylor would not be persuaded. "I will," he said, "by God's grace, go and appear before them, and to their beards resist their false doing." In a day or two he departed, leaving his parish in charge of "a godly old priest," Richard Yeoman, who soon after suffered martyrdom at Norwich. Arriving at London, he presented himself before Gardiner. At the close of their interview he was committed to King's Bench prison, where he remained almost two years. After several examinations he was finally condemned. On the fourth of February, 1555, Edward Bonner, bishop of London, of infamous memory as a persecutor, came to his prison to degrade him. Bonner promised Dr. Taylor if he would recant, a pardon, and that "he would do well enough." He had been previously tempted with a bishopric. Dr. Taylor, refusing, was, after the usual ceremonies, declared to be no longer a priest. On the same evening his wife and son were allowed to pay him a short visit. As soon as they came in, all kneeled down and repeated the Litany. The remaining time was occupied by him in affectionate counsels. On parting, he presented to his wife a copy of the Book of Common Prayer, as authorized in King Edward's reign, and to his son "a Latin book containing the notable sayings of the old martyrs, gathered out of the Ecclesiastical History," on the fly-leaf of which he had written his last will. He signed it "Rowland Taylor, departing hence in sure hope, without all doubting of eternal salvation, I thank God my heavenly Father, through Jesus Christ my certain Saviour." At two o'clock the same night the sheriff of London with his men came and removed Dr. Taylor to the Woolpack inn. Mrs. Taylor, anticipating this, had meanwhile kept watch all night in the porch of St. Botolph's church, with her two daughters. The affecting scene, with others which are to follow, cannot be better told than in the simple and beautiful record of John Fox's *Book of Martyrs.*

"Now, when the sheriff and his company came against St. Botolph's church, Elizabeth cried, saying, 'O my dear father; mother, mother, here is my father led away!' Then his wife said, 'Rowland, Rowland, where art thou?' For it was a very dark morning, that the one could not see the other. Dr. Taylor answered, 'Dear wife, I am here, and stayed.' The sheriff's men would have led him forth, but the sheriff said, 'Stay a little, masters, I pray you, and let him speak to his wife,' and so they stayed.

"Then she came to him, and he took his

daughter Mary in his arms, and he, his wife, and Elizabeth, kneeled down and said the Lord's Prayer. At which sight the sheriff wept apace, and so did several others of the company. After they had prayed, he rose up and kissed his wife, and shook her by the hand, and said, 'Farewell, my dear wife; be of good comfort, for I am quiet in my conscience. God shall stir up a father for my children.' And then he kissed his daughter Mary, and said, 'God bless thee, and make thee his servant:' and kissing Elizabeth, he said, 'God bless thee. I pray you all stand steadfast unto Christ and His Word, and keep you from idolatry.' Then, said his wife, 'God be with thee, dear Rowland; I will with God's grace meet thee at Hadley.'"

Dr. Taylor remained at the Woolpack until eleven o'clock, when he was taken in charge by the sheriff of Essex county, and the party left the inn on horseback. As they passed the gate, which had been closed to exclude the people, they found Thomas, Dr. Taylor's son, with his faithful servant, John Hull. "When Dr. Taylor saw them, he called them, saying, 'Come hither, my son Thomas.' And John Hull lifted the child up and set him on the horse before his father: and Dr. Taylor put off his hat, and said to the people that stood there looking on him, 'Good people, this is mine own son, begotten of my body in lawful matrimony; and God be blessed for lawful matrimony.' Then he lifted up his eyes towards heaven and prayed for his son; laid his hand upon the child's head and blessed him, and so delivered the child to John Hull, whom he took by the hand and said, 'Farewell, John Hull, the faithfullest servant that ever man had.' And so they rode forth." As they proceeded, they covered Dr. Taylor's head and face with a close hood, with slits before the eyes, that he might not be recognized.

"All the way," the chronicle continues, "Dr. Taylor was joyful and merry, as one that accounted himself going to a most pleasant banquet or marriage. He spake many notable things to the sheriff and yeomen of the guard that conducted him, and often moved them to weep through his much earnest calling upon them to repent, and to amend their evil and wicked living. Oftentimes also he caused them to wonder and rejoice, to see him so constant and steadfast, void of all fear, joyful in heart, and glad to die."

At Chelmsford, Dr. Taylor was delivered to the sheriff of Suffolk county, who accompanied him to Hadley. The party remained two days at Lanham, where they were joined by "a great number of gentlemen and justices upon great horses, which all were appointed to aid the sheriff." These gentlemen endeavored to induce Dr. Taylor to recant, promising him if he would do so, his pardon, which they held ready, and an appointment to a bishopric, but without success.

As they entered Hadley, they found a poor man with five small children, who, as soon as he saw Dr. Taylor, knelt down with his children, "and cried with a loud voice, 'O dear father and good shepherd, Dr. Taylor, God help and succor thee, as thou hast many a time succored me and my poor children.'" As they passed along, the streets "were beset on both sides the way with men and women of the town and country, who waited to see him; whom when they beheld so led to death, with weeping eyes and lamentable voices they cried, saying one to another, 'Ah, good Lord! there goeth our good shepherd from us, that so faithfully hath taught us, so fatherly hath cared for us, and so godly hath governed us: O merciful God! what shall we poor scattered lambs do? What shall come of this most wicked world? Good Lord strengthen him and comfort him;' with such other most lamentable and piteous voices. Wherefore the people were sore rebuked by the sheriff and catchpoles his men, that led him. And Dr. Taylor always said to the people, 'I have preached to you God's word and truth, and am come this day to seal it with my blood.'"

As he passed the alms-houses, a row of small tenements, each occupied by a separate family, he distributed to the people at the doors the little money remaining of that which he had himself received in alms,—his living having been taken from him when he was first imprisoned, and his support having been since derived entirely from the gifts of charitable persons who visited him.

As he came to the last alms-house, "not seeing the poor that dwelt there ready at their doors as the others were, he asked, 'Is the blind man and blind woman that dwelt here alive?' It was answered, 'Yea, they are within.' Then he threw the glove (which he had used as a purse) and all in at the window, and so rode forth."

When he came to Aldham Common, where he was to suffer, he exclaimed, "Thanked be God, I am even at home," and alighting from his horse, tore off his hood. As the people, assembled in great multitude, "saw his reverend and ancient face, with a long white beard, they burst out with weeping tears, and cried, saying, 'God save thee, good Dr. Taylor; Jesus Christ strengthen thee, and help thee; the Holy Ghost comfort thee;' with such other like good wishes." He attempted to speak to the people, but one or another of the guard, thrusting a staff into his mouth, prevented him. He then appealed to the sheriff, who reminded him of his promise to the Council. "Well," said Dr. Taylor, "promise must be kept." The agreement is not known, but the common report at the time was, that after the condemnation of himself and others, the Council had threatened that they would cut out the prisoners' tongues, unless they promised not to address the people at the time of their execution. Like the wicked rulers of olden time, these tyrants "feared the people." Finding that he could not speak, he sat down, and called to one Joyce, "I pray thee, come and pull off my boots, and take them for thy labor; thou hast long looked for them, now take them." Putting off all but his shirt, he cried with a loud voice, "Good people, I have taught you nothing but God's holy Word; and those lessons that I have taken out of God's blessed book, the Holy Bible; and I am come hither this day to seal it with my blood." Here he was interrupted by a brutal guard, who struck him on the head. He then knelt down and prayed. "A poor woman that was among the people, pushed forward and knelt with him. She was thrust away and threatened to be trampled down by the horses, but was not to be forced away."

His prayer ended, Dr. Taylor went to the stake, kissed it, and then placing himself in a pitch barrel which had been provided, stood upright, "with his hands folded together, and his eyes towards heaven, and so he continually prayed."

He was then bound with chains; and the sheriff ordered Richard Donningham to set up the fagots, but he refused to do so, saying, "I am lame, sir, and not able to lift a fagot." He was threatened with prison, but still refused. Four others were appointed "to set up the fagots, and to make the fire, which they most diligently did." One of them, a ruffian, threw a fagot in Dr. Taylor's face, wounding him. "O friend," said the martyr, "I have harm enough, what needed that?"

As he continued his devotions, repeating the Psalm *Miserere* in English, one Sir John Shelton struck him on the lips, saying, "Ye knave, speak Latin; I will make thee."

"At last they kindled the fire; and Dr. Taylor, holding up both his hands, called upon God, and said, 'Merciful Father of heaven, for Jesus Christ my Saviour's sake, receive my soul into thy hands.' So stood he still without either crying or moving, with his hands folded together, till Joyce, with a halberd, struck him on the head that the brains fell out, and the corpse fell down into the fire.

"Thus rendered the man of God his blessed soul into the hands of his merciful Father, and to his most dear and certain Saviour Jesus Christ, whom he most entirely loved, faithfully and earnestly preached, obediently followed in living, and constantly glorified in death."

CHAPTER II.

JEREMY TAYLOR'S FATHER—NOBLE ANCESTRY—POSITION OF A BARBER—BIRTHPLACE—A YOUNG PUPIL—ENTERS CAIUS COLLEGE—BAPTISM—A SIZAR—DOMESTIC RELATIONS—MILTON—FELLOWSHIP AND DEGREES—ORDINATION—PREACHES AT ST. PAUL'S—HIS SUCCESS—ARCHBISHOP LAUD—YOUTH—ELECTED FELLOW AT OXFORD.

THE exact date of the birth of Jeremy Taylor is not known. He was baptized on the fifteenth day of August, 1613. His father, Nathaniel Taylor, was a barber. Notwithstanding his humble calling and limited means, he could boast an ancestry nobler than that of many titled families. He was a descendant from Dr. Rowland Taylor, the confessor for the faith of the Church of England. No post of military fame, no service for country, could entail as great a glory as this enlistment in "the noble army of martyrs." No herald's cunning could illuminate so bright an escutcheon as the reflected blaze of the fire at Hadley.

The calling of a barber was more important at that time than of late years. Many minor operations of surgery, such as blood-letting and tooth-drawing, were committed to his care; a practice still continued in countries which, like Spain for instance, seem to have known no growth of a social nature for the past two centuries. Taking all this into account, however, it was still an humble station, and the advancement of Jeremy Taylor, like that of many other great men in English history, teaches the republican doctrine, that "Honor and shame from no condition rise."

Two houses, still in existence, claim to have been the birthplace of Jeremy Taylor. Both are now occupied as inns. One, with a sign of slightly academic suggestiveness, "The Wrestlers," is in the street called the Petty Cury; the other, with the bluff and brief name of "The Black Bear,"* is opposite Trinity church, and seems to have the best claim to the coveted distinction.

We find Mr. Taylor filling, in 1621, the office of Churchwarden; and we learn from a letter by his son, written some time after, that he was reasonably learned, "and had solely grounded his children in mathematics." He

---

* *Gentleman's Magazine*, April, 1855, p. 377.

took early care for the education of his son Jeremy, for we find the child, in 1616, one of the pupils of a free-school endowed by the bequest of Dr. Stephen Perse, Senior Fellow of Caius College. Jeremy must have been one of the earliest beneficiaries, and the trust have been administered with exemplary promptitude, for the death of Dr. Perse occurred only the year before.

The pupil doubtless made rapid progress, notwithstanding his tender age, for we find him ten years later, entered at Caius College on the eighteenth of August, 1626. He is stated in the college admission-book to have been in his fifteenth year. In the funeral sermon by his friend Bishop Rust, he is said to have entered "by the time he was thirteen years old." The latter authority, that of a personal friend, has been followed by the Bishop's biographers. The latest of these, Mr. Willmott, however, suggests that as we possess only the date of Taylor's baptism, we cannot positively convict the register of error. A passage in one of his writings shows that baptism was at the period usually administered soon after birth. "We are," says Dr. Taylor, "born of Christian parents, made Christians at ten days old." Jeremy Taylor is entered as "Filius Nathanielis Tayloris, tonsoris Cantabrigiæ," so that his father still continued his avocation of barber. The young student entered college as a sizar. A sizar was one who received the same education with those of greater means, but was expected to perform a few of the offices of a servant, such as waiting at table. Bishop Heber has shown in his *Life of Taylor*, that the practice must be judged by the simple manners of the age which witnessed its origin, when duties of the class required of the sizar were willingly paid, as they are to some extent to this day, by the lord to the sovereign, and by the vassal to the lord. Master and servant in those old times, as in many of our farm-houses at the present time, took their meals together at the long table in the old hall, and were associated in like manner in many other scenes of domestic routine.

Jeremy Taylor, for a portion of his collegiate course, was a fellow-student of John Milton. The poet had entered Christ's College in the year 1625. There is no record of any intimacy between the two, and the active part which they took on opposite sides in the great contest which occupied so large a portion of their lives, prevented the intercourse which might have been naturally anticipated between the master of prose and the master of verse. Milton is, however, known to have been through life a great reader and admirer of Dr. Taylor's eloquent writings.

An examination of the books of Caius College, by "A Caius Man," who has communicated the results of his searches to the public in the pages of the *Gentleman's Magazine*,* shows Jeremy Taylor to have remained a sizar for nearly two years. He then received one of the scholarships founded by Dr. Perse, and retained this position for five years, when he was made a Fellow. The college records contain the names of several undergraduates instructed by him. Among these we find the name of Edward Landisdale, who is supposed to be the same person who afterwards became Dr. Taylor's brother-in-law.

He received his degree of Master of Arts about the same time with his Fellowship, and was soon after ordained, before he was twenty-one years of age.

---

* *Gentleman's Magazine*, April, 1855.

The young clergyman was at once placed prominently before the public. His college room-mate, or "chum," as the relation was then as now familiarly expressed, Mr. Risden, who had been appointed lecturer at St. Paul's Cathedral, invited his former associate to occupy his pulpit for a short period. Bishop Rust records the young divine's success in enthusiastic terms. "He preached to the admiration and astonishment of his auditory, and by his florid and youthful beauty, and sweet and pleasant air, and sublime and raised discourses, he made his hearers take him for some young angel, newly descended from the visions of glory." The language is extravagant, but when we recall the florid eloquence of Taylor's published writings, and which no doubt pervaded to an even less restrained degree these early compositions, and consider the effect of such words from a speaker whose countenance, even when marked by the care and study of after years, retained convincing proof of early beauty, heightened by an habitual grace of manner and melody of voice, we cannot but receive its testimony as truthful.

The fame of these discourses soon reached the ears of Archbishop Laud, who invited the young divine to preach at his chapel at Lambeth. "He performed the task," Bishop Rust informs us, "not less to the Archbishop's wonder than satisfaction: his discourse was beyond exception, and beyond imitation. The wise prelate," Rust continues, "thought him too young, but the great youth humbly begged his grace to pardon that fault, and promised, if he lived, he would mend it." The sprightly reply probably helped to confirm the Archbishop's good opinion, but he wisely persevered in his endeavor to withdraw the youth from a too early public career, thinking it "for the advantage of the world that such mighty parts should be afforded better opportunities of study and improvement than a course of constant preaching would allow of."

It is not known whether Mr. Taylor, after this interview, returned to Cambridge, or, according to a tradition mentioned by Bishop Heber, pursued his studies in some country retirement. He resigned his Fellowship at Cambridge in 1636, and on the twentieth of October in the same year, was admitted a Master of Arts in University College, Oxford. He was proposed ten days after as a Fellow. Although candidates were required by the statutes to have been connected with the university for three years, he received a majority of the votes cast; but the Warden, or head of the college, refused to take part in the election. In consequence of this, the Fellows persisting in their choice, no election took place, and the appointment passed into the hands of the Archbishop, as Visitor of the college. As Mr. Taylor's change of residence and nomination had been effected at the prelate's request, he exercised his privilege by appointing his friend to the vacant place.

CHAPTER III.

CHAPLAIN TO THE ARCHBISHOP—FRANCIS À SANCTA CLARA —CHRISTOPHER AND JOHN DAVENPORT—THE CHARGE OF ROMANISM—SERMON ON THE GUNPOWDER PLOT— MARRIAGE—LETTER TO DR. LANGSDALE—ITS DATE— VOWS IN SICKNESS—CHILDREN.

MR. TAYLOR was soon after appointed one of the Archbishop's chaplains. This was followed, on the 23d of March, 1637, by a presentation by Dr. Juxon, bishop of London, probably through the influence of the Archbishop, to the Rectory of Uppingham, in Rutlandshire. The duties connected with the chaplaincy and the parish of course led to frequent absences from the university. Little is known respecting the four years of his fellowship. He is said by Anthony à Wood, to have been charged with a leaning to Romanism. The rumor appears to have arisen from his intimacy with a learned Franciscan friar, known as Francis à Sancta Clara. An interesting account of this remarkable personage is given by Bishop Heber. His real name was Christopher Davenport. Born of Protestant parents, he was entered, at the age of fifteen, with his brother John, as a *battler*, or poor scholar, at Merton College, Oxford, in the year 1613. The brothers separated widely in their religious opinions. John became a Puritan and afterwards an Independent. Christopher, after passing two years at Merton, fled to the French College of Douay, with a Roman Catholic priest, where he joined the Franciscan order. After wandering for several years among the universities of the Low Countries and Spain he returned to England, where he was made one of Queen Henrietta's chaplains, and labored earnestly though quietly for fifty years in the service of his church. He is said by Wood to have been much esteemed "by many great and worthy persons." His numerous works are for the most part moderate in tone, too much so to suit the tastes of the authorities of Rome, since we find one of his productions, *Deus, Natura, Gratia*, on the *Index Expurgatorius* in Spain, and narrowly escaping a public burning in Italy. He became, after the Restoration, principal chaplain to the queen of Charles the Second, and provincial of his order in England. He made many friends at Oxford, where he frequently took shelter from his opponents, and died at a great age, in 1680, at London.

The society of this well-furnished scholar, of such varied experience, was doubtless attractive. A charge similar to that brought against Taylor was made against the Archbishop upon his trial. Both were without foundation, but they are noteworthy as instances of a slander which seems to be of periodical recurrence in every season of active Protestant discussion. The charge clung to Dr. Taylor through life, notwithstanding his repeated condemnation of Romish error in the rapid succession of his published works.

Wood, in support of this early charge of Romanist tendencies, tells us that Taylor having been appointed to preach on the anniversary of the Gunpowder Plot, the Vice-chancellor insisted on inserting many passages highly offensive to the Roman Catholics, and that after the delivery of the discourse, the preacher expressed his regret for these expressions to his Franciscan friend. The sermon, which has been published, is a refutation of the first part of the story. It presents a connected argument, exhibiting the consistency of the Romish system with intrigue and plot, so interwoven with the entire composition that it could not have been introduced at the suggestion of another, without rewriting the whole. As regards the latter portion, the preacher may, it is well suggested by Mr. Willmott, have made an apology for the tone of his remarks, without possessing the least sympathy with the views of his opponent.

His denial of the charge in a letter to a friend, on a subsequent revival of the slander, is clear and emphatic: "Sir, that party which need such lying stories for the support of their cause, proclaim their cause to be very weak, or themselves to be very evil advocates. Sir, be confident, they dare not tempt me to do so, and it is not the *first* time they have endeavored to serve their ends by saying such things of me. But, I bless God for it, it is perfectly a slander, and it shall, I hope, for ever prove so."

Our next record is one in pleasant contrast with strife and contention. Mr. Taylor, then in his twenty-sixth year, was married, on the twenty-seventh of May, 1639, in his church at Uppingham, to Phebe Langsdale. Nothing is known of the lady's family except from a letter by her husband, preserved in the British Museum, addressed "To my very dear brother, Dr. Langsdale, at his Apothecary's House in Gainsborough." The handwriting, Mr. Willmott informs us, is "of peculiar neatness, recalling the delicate characters of Gray." The letter presents an admirable picture of "brethren in unity," and contains equally admirable counsel of universal application. Dr. Langsdale afterwards removed to Leeds, where he was buried, January 7, 1683.

Dear Brother,

Thy letter was most welcome to me, bringing the happy news of thy recovery. I had notice of thy danger, but watched for this happy relation, and had laid wait with Royston to inquire of Mr. Rumbould. I hope I shall not need to bid thee be careful for the perfecting thy health and to be fearful of a relapse, though I am very much, yet thou thyself art more concerned in it. But this I will remind thee of, that thou be infinitely [careful] to perform to God all those holy promises which I suppose thou didst make in thy sickness, and remember what thoughts thou hadst then, and bear them along upon thy spirit all thy lifetime; for that which was true then, is so still; and the world is really as vain a thing, as thou didst then suppose it. I durst not tell thy mother of thy danger (though I heard of it), till at the same time I told her of thy recovery. Poor woman! she was troubled and pleased at the same time; but your letter did determine her. I take it kindly that thou hast writ to Bowman. If I had been in condition, you should not have been troubled with it, but, as it is, thou and I must be content. Thy mother sends her blessing to her and her little Mally; so do I, and my prayers to God for you both. Your little cousins are your servants, and I am thy most affectionate and endeared brother,

November 24, 1643. JER. TAYLOR.

There is a doubt respecting the date of this letter. The writer in the Gentleman's Magazine whom we have already cited, states that the original appears "on reference to the MS. (No. 4274, § 125), to have been dated, November 24, 1653, in the same somewhat faded ink as the body of the letter. But on the 5 has been written 4 in darker ink."

The question of course arises as to the period

of this alteration. The "Caius Man" inclines to the supposition that it is a modern alteration, from the fact that the letter is registered in the "Catalogue of original Letters and other Autographs," prefixed to the volume by its collector Thoresby, under 1653. If this date is adopted, we may suppose the "little cousins" at the close of the letter to have been Mr. Taylor's two children, the word at that time having the general meaning of relation. "Little Mally" was Dr. Langsdale's daughter, and afterwards became Mrs. Mary Potter.*

Mr. Taylor had three sons by this marriage. The youngest of these, William, died on the 28th of May, 1642, and was followed soon after by his mother. The two remaining sons grew to man's estate, but preceded their father, though by no long interval, to the grave.

---

* *Gentleman's Magazine*, April, 1855.

CHAPTER IV.

THE CROWN AND PARLIAMENT—THE CHURCH OF ENGLAND UNDER HENRY VIII., EDWARD VI., MARY, AND ELIZABETH —JAMES I.—THE CONFERENCE—POINTS OF DIFFERENCE —CHARLES I.—THE LITURGY IN SCOTLAND—WAR WITH THE SCOTS—IMPEACHMENT OF LAUD AND STRAFFORD— ACTS OF PARLIAMENT—NOTTINGHAM—TAYLOR JOINS THE KING'S ARMY—OXFORD TITLES—UPPINGHAM PARISH—ISAAC MASSEY—DR. TAYLOR'S IMPRISONMENT—HIS ALLUSIONS TO MILITARY AFFAIRS—THE TROOPER—THE SOLDIER IN A BREACH.

THE long struggle between the Crown and Parliament is one of the most important passages in English history. It is impossible for us, within our present limits, to convey any adequate idea of the great contest; but it is at the same time necessary to put the reader in possession, to some extent, of the state of affairs which summoned Jeremy Taylor from his quiet parish duties and the delights of study, to the rude and stirring life of the camp.

The English nation seem to have very gen

erally acquiesced in the Reformation under Henry VIII., and the arrangement of the Liturgy and constitution of the Church during the brief reign of Edward VI. The relapse to Popery under Mary, while it strengthened the hold of the Reformers upon the affections of the people, by the testimony sealed with blood at the many martyr fires throughout the land, sowed seeds of evil which were not developed until the reign of her successor. The Marian persecution drove many of the reformed clergy to the Continent, where they became acquainted with a class of learned and excellent men, who carried their opposition to Popery so far as violently to denounce Episcopacy, clerical vestments, the use of a liturgy, the sign of the cross in baptism, and other matters regarded in England as indispensable to the permanence and good order of the Church. They returned to their native country, when the Church of England was restored to power, to urge these views. A law requiring entire uniformity in religious worship, passed soon after, probably tended to exasperate this party and, as is usually the case with any legislation which can be charged with persecution, to increase its numbers. While affairs were in this angry state Elizabeth died, and James the First ascended the throne.

One of the first acts of the new monarch was to summon a conference for the settlement of religious opinions and observances. It was, however, conducted by the King with such outrageous disregard to the party of objectors, that the great opportunity for conciliation was lost, and matters became worse than before. The King was narrow minded and despotic. The zeal of the Bishops unfortunately identified the Church of England with this false policy. Naturally desirous to establish uniformity of ritual observance, they fell into the error, common in that age to all forms of religious belief, of supposing that this could be effected by force. Had they adopted the tolerant practice of the Church at the present day, especially in this country, the unhappy divisions which now disgrace the Protestant cause might have been prevented. The non-conformists had not yet become dissenters. They acquiesced very generally in the rule of bishops and the use of the Liturgy. It really seems strange that the chief points of difference were the use of the surplice and episcopal robe, the cross in baptism, the ring in matrimony, the bowing in the creed, the kneeling at the sacrament. In this country, none of these things have ever been enforced, and the consequence has been that their inherent beauty and fitness have quietly led to their universal adoption within the Episcopal ranks.

The King's weak love of rule soon brought him into difficulties with his Parliament, and this forced him to various mean shifts to raise money without their sanction. He was too timid to suffer affairs to come to an open rupture, but his frequent concessions being followed by renewed attempts to tyrannize, their good effect was entirely lost.

During this distracted state of affairs James was succeeded by his son Charles. The new monarch, reared in a bad school, made similar mistakes of an arbitrary character at the outset of his reign. Opposed by Parliament, he at last determined to rule without its support. He persevered in this unwise course for several years, raising money by various pretexts, and endeavoring to enforce religious conformity by the strong arm of power. By the advice of Archbishop Laud a liturgy was prepared for Scotland. On the day of its introduction a riot interrupted the services at

St. Giles' church, Edinburgh. The Solemn League and Covenant, an agreement to support the Presbyterianism which had held nearly undisputed sway since the time of John Knox, received many signatures. The King raised an army and entered Scotland to subdue the revolt. A compromise was effected and the King returned. He had scarcely done so, when the Scottish Parliament and General Assembly voted Episcopacy unlawful, and the High Commission Court, a recently established tribunal, tyrannical. The Parliament was prorogued before these measures could become laws. The King determined to send a second army. As his means were exhausted, and in the present temper of the nation he could not venture on any irregular expedient to raise money, he was compelled to summon Parliament.

Parliament met on the 13th of April, 1640. It was foolishly dissolved by the King on the fifth of May. He resorted to money-lenders, and obtaining a supply advanced against the Scots. His army was defeated at Newburn, and a dishonorable truce effected. He was now compelled again to summon Parliament. One of the first acts of that body was to impeach the king's chief counsellors, Archbishop Laud, and Thomas Wentworth, earl of Strafford, of high treason. Both were committed to prison, and Strafford, having been convicted, was, with the king's consent, beheaded. These and other measures appeased the opposition, and the king's popularity was returning, when by an absurd attempt to arrest several members of Parliament, he again aroused distrust and discontent. Acts were passed, excluding bishops from the House of Peers, and for raising forces. Both of these were approved by the King. A bill was next passed appointing the commanding officers of the different counties, and making them responsible to the Parliament instead of the King. This measure the monarch resisted. He finally sct up his standard at Nottingham, August 22, 1642, calling upon all his subjects to come to his support against the Parliament. Taylor, who had been appointed one of the king's chaplains about the same time that he had received the living of Uppingham, was now summoned from its peaceful seclusion to the camp, and was one of the first to join the royal forces. His recent domestic bereavements probably combined with his royalist sympathies in urging him to this step. The entries in the parish register in his handwriting cease after the summer of 1642. As the line of march of the royal army from Nottingham to Oxford passed near his parish, it is probable that he then joined the ranks. The King, after entering Oxford, advanced as far as Colnbrook on the way to London, but fearful of engaging with the large force raised by Parliament to meet him returned to the university, where he resided for some time in Christ Church College. On the first of November in the same year, a convocation of the university authorities was held, and at the King's request Mr. Taylor received the degree of D. D. from this assembly. The honor was however lessened by the indiscriminate manner in which this and other academic titles were conferred, by royal command, on many persons who had taken part in recent engagements, or identified themselves with the royal cause. Titles of this class were now almost the only honors in the King's gift, and were so lavishly bestowed as to call forth a remonstrance from the university.

An act, passed on the fifteenth of October by Parliament, that the revenues "of such notorious delinquents as had taken up arms against the Parliament, or had been active in the commission of array, should be sequestered for the use and service of the Commonwealth," now deprived Taylor of all income arising from his parish. No one, however, appears to have been regularly appointed to, or a claimant for, the vacant parish, until 1661, the year Dr. Taylor became a bishop, when we find John Allington signing himself "rector there." The parish was, in the mean time, supplied with a Puritan lecturer. A curious passage in the *Mercurius Aulicus*, one of the earliest forerunners of the modern newspaper, for the week ending May 2, 1644, presents a far from flattering picture of this successor of Mr. Taylor. The writer, in the course of his remarks on the clergy favored by the Parliament, says:

"Monday, May 6.—Now if you would see what heavenly men these lecturers are, be pleased to take notice, that at Uppingham, in Rutlandshire, the members have placed one Isaac Massey to teach the people (for the true pastor, Dr. Jeremy Taylor, for his learning and loyalty, is driven thence, his house plundered, his estate seized, and his family driven out of doors). This Massey, at a Communion this last Easter, having consecrated the bread after his manner, laid one hand upon the chalice, and smiting his breast with the other, said to the parishioners: 'As I am a faithful sinner, neighbors, this is my morning draught;' and turning himself round to them, said, 'Neighbors, here's to ye all!' and so drank off the whole cupful, which is none of the least. Many of the parish were hereby scandalized, and therefore departed without receiving the Sacrament. Among which, one old man, seeing Massey drink after this manner, said aloud, 'Sir, much good do it you.' Whereupon Massey replied, 'Thou blessest with thy tongue, and cursest with thy heart; but 'tis no matter, for God will bless whom thou cursest.' This Massey, coming lately into a house of the town, used these words, 'This town of Uppingham loves Popery, and we would reform it, but they will not' (and without any further coherence, said): 'but I say, whoever says there is any king in England besides the Parliament at Westminster, I'll make him for ever speaking more.' The master of the house replied, 'I say there is a king in England besides the Parliament in Westminster;' whereupon Massey, with his cudgel, broke the gentleman's head. Whoever doubts that Mr. Massey is injured by these relations, may satisfy themselves by inquiring of the inhabitants of Uppingham parish."

The *Mercurius Aulicus* was issued, and for the most part written, by Sir John Birkenhead, a leading member of the Royalist party. As he was acquainted with Dr. Taylor, it is surmised by Mr. Willmott, to whom we are indebted for this curious extract, that the information may have been supplied by the ejected rector. The cool reference to the best witnesses in the case, the people of the parish, at the close of the narrative, shows that the writer was prepared to substantiate his testimony, however obtained, if questioned as that of a partisan, by ample proof.

Dr. Taylor is supposed to have been with the royal forces before Gloucester and at Newbury. The ill success of these movements forced the king to return to Oxford. On the fourth of February of the following year, Dr. Taylor is mentioned as one of the prisoners taken by the parliamentary troops after their victory over Colonel Charles Gerard before Cardigan Castle. His imprisonment was not probably of long duration, as we find him in the fall of the same year at Oxford. He does not appear to have again joined the army.

The stirring scenes of a campaign must have vividly impressed themselves upon his active imagination, and traces of this portion of his career are, as might naturally be supposed, scattered through his writings. Numerous passages of this description have been collected by Mr. Willmott. The following companion pictures are evidently from the life. Often as the subjects have been treated, they have never been more vividly brought before us by pen or pencil.

The first, in the sermon entitled "The Apples of Sodom," is a comparison of the sinner roused, after having yielded to temptation, to the consequences, which in the excitement of the act he had forgotten.

"But so have I known a bold trooper fight in the confusion of a battle, and, being warm with heat and rage, receive from the sword of his enemy wounds open like a grave; but he felt them not; and when, by the streams of blood, he found himself marked for pain, he refused to consider then what he was to feel to-morrow; but when his rage hath cooled into the temper of a man, and clammy moisture hath checked the fiery emission of spirits, he wonders at his own boldness, and blames his fate, and needs a mighty patience to bear his great calamity."

The second passage occurs in *Holy Dying*. "And what can we complain of the weakness of our strengths, or the pressures of diseases, when we see a poor soldier stand in a breach, almost starved* with cold and hunger, and his cold apt to be relieved only by the heats of anger, a fever, or a fired musket, and his hunger slacked by a greater pain or a huge fear? This man shall stand in his arms and wounds, pale and faint, weary and watchful; and at night shall have a bullet pulled out of his flesh, and shivers from his bones, and endure his mouth to be sewed up from a violent rent to its own dimensions."

---

* Used in its primitive meaning of *killed*.

CHAPTER V.

EPISCOPACY ASSERTED—TOLERATION—SIR CHRISTOPHER HATTON—DUGDALE—THE DIRECTORY—APOLOGY FOR THE LITURGY—THE PSALTER—THE CIVIL WAR—KING DAVID—CHURCH UNION—RETIREMENT IN WALES—REMARRIAGE—NICHOLSON AND WYATT—NEWTON HALL—POWELL AND LLOYD—GRAMMAR—HATTON THE YOUNGER—INTERVIEW WITH CHARLES I.—LIBERTY OF PROPHESYING—TOLERATION—ABRAHAM AND HIS GUEST.

MR. TAYLOR, soon after joining the King at Oxford, published a work entitled *Episcopacy Asserted against the Acephali and Aerians, New and Old.* It was prepared at the request of the King, as a defence of the views of the Church of England respecting Church government. The author derives the Episcopal office from that of the Apostles,*

---

* He states this in strong terms in his dedication. "Episcopacy relies not upon the authority of fathers and councils, but upon Scripture; upon the institution of Christ, or the institution of the Apostles; upon a universal tradition and a universal practice, not upon the words and opinions of the doctors: it hath as great a testimony as Scripture itself hath."

and clearly points out its pre-eminence and authority from the earliest ages of the Church. It is written in a clear and vigorous style, and with the tone of moderation towards those of different views which honorably distinguishes all his writings. He expressly denies the right of coercion in religious belief. "As no human power," he says, "can disrobe the Church of the power of excommunication, so no human power can invest the Church with a lay compulsory. For, if the Church be not capable of a '*jus gladii*,' as most certainly she is not, the Church cannot receive power to put men to death, or to inflict lesser pains in order to it, or any thing above a salutary penance."

The work is dedicated to Christopher Hatton, Esq., afterwards Lord Hatton of Kirby, a gentleman of worth residing near Uppingham. He was a liberal friend of learning, and rendered an important service to the history of his native country by encouraging and aiding the celebrated antiquarian, Dugdale, in his visits to the most important cathedrals, parish churches, and religious establishments of the kingdom. Dugdale copied various inscriptions and armorial bearings from tombs and windows during the summer of 1641, and his rec-

5*

ord is in many cases the only one in existence of much that was soon after wantonly destroyed by the Puritans.

On the first of July, 1643, the Assembly of Divines, in whose charge the management of ecclesiastical affairs was now placed, issued a work entitled *A Directory for the Public Worship of God throughout the Three Kingdoms of England, Scotland, and Ireland.* It contains a number of suggestions and directions respecting the matter and manner of extempore prayers. Its use was enforced by an Act of Parliament, "for the taking away of the Book of Common Prayer, and for establishing and observing of this present Directory throughout the kingdom of England and dominion of Wales." Dr. Taylor met this by the preparation of his *Apology for Authorized and Set Forms of Liturgy, against the Pretence of the Spirit.* His work appeared anonymously in 1646, with the title, *A Discourse concerning Prayer Extempore, or by Pretence of the Spirit, in Justification of Authorized and Set Forms of Liturgy.* The work reappeared in its present enlarged form, and with its present title, in the same year, with a dedication to the king. A third edition followed three years later, in which the author gave a significant proof of his disinterested respect for the monarch by retaining the original inscription.

This work is divided into two portions: the first answering the objections of those who disapprove of all forms of devotion, the second addressed to those who, sensible of some of the advantages of a liturgy, object to being bound to its use on all occasions of public worship. In the preface he has considered the merits of the Book of Common Prayer. Dr. Taylor's opinion on these topics is the more valuable, as the ease and eloquence of his own devotional writings show that he could have easily excelled in extempore prayer, had he deemed it fitting to use public devotion as a means of personal display. His published sermons close in many instances with an original prayer, as was then the custom of divines, but the prayer was evidently, like the sermon, carefully composed in advance of the occasion for its use.

In 1644, a volume was published at Oxford with the title, *The Psalter of David, with Titles and Collects according to the matter of each Psalm, by the Right Honorable Christopher Hatton.* The "titles and collects" are from the pen of Dr. Taylor, and the work appeared in the eighth edition, 1672, with his name as author. Each collect contains a summary of the contents of the psalm which precedes it, expressed with the author's wonted grace and fervor. No reason is known for the substitution of his friend Hatton's name for his own on the original title-page.

The preface contains a passage of interest from its personal nature. "In this most unnatural war commenced against the greatest solemnities of Christianity, and all that is called God, I have been put to it to run somewhither to sanctuary; but whither, was so great a question, that had not religion been my guide, I had not known where to have found rest or safety: when the King and the laws, who, by God and man respectively, are appointed the protectors of innocence and truth, had themselves the greatest need of a protector. And when, in the beginning of these troubles, I hastened to his Majesty, the case of the King and his good subjects was something like that of Isaac ready to be sacrificed; the wood was prepared, the fire kindled, the knife was lift up, and the hand was striking; that, if we had not been something like

Abraham too, and 'against hope had believed in hope,' we had been as much without comfort, as we were, in outward appearance, without remedy.

"It was my custom long since to secure myself against the violence of discontents abroad, —as Gerson did against temptations,—'*in angulis et libellis*,' 'in my books and my retirements;' but now I was deprived of both them, and driven to a public view and participation of those dangers and miseries which threatened the kingdom, and disturbed the evenness of my former life. I was, therefore, constrained to amass together all those arguments of hope and comfort, by which men in the like condition were supported; and amongst all the great examples of trouble and confidence, I reckoned King David one of the biggest, and of greatest consideration. For, considering that he was a king vexed with a civil war, his case had so much of ours in it, that it was likely the devotions he used might fit our turn, and his comforts sustain us."

Another passage shows his chief aim in the preparation of the work to have been the promotion of the noble cause of Catholic union. After showing that the recorded devotions of our Saviour and the Apostles, are, almost entirely, taken from Psalms, he says, "I thought I might not imprudently intend this book as an instrument of public charity to Christians of different confessions. For I see that all sorts of people sing or say David's Psalms; and by that use, if they understand the consequences of their own religion, accept set forms of prayer for their liturgy, and this form in special is one of their own choices for devotion: so that if all Christians that think David's Psalms lawful devotions, and shall observe the collects from them to be just of the same religion, would join in this or the like form, I am something confident the product would be charity, besides other spiritual advantages. For my own particular, since all Christendom is so much divided and subdivided into innumerable sects, I knew not how to give a better evidence of my own belief and love of the communion of saints, and detestation of schism, than by an act of religion, whose consequence might be, if men please, the advancement of a universal communion."

The exact date of Dr. Taylor's retirement from the army is unknown. All hope of success for the royal arms was now at an end.

Dr. Taylor, as we have seen, had been taken prisoner in Wales. After his release he seems to have established himself in that portion of the country. A celebrated passage in the introduction to *The Liberty of Prophesying*, evidently refers to this portion of his career, and furnishes almost our only information respecting it.

"In the great storm," he says, "which dashed the vessel of the Church in pieces, I was cast on the coast of Wales; and in a little boat, thought to have enjoyed that rest and quietness which in England I could not hope for. Here I cast anchor; and thinking to ride safely, the storm followed me with so impetuous a violence, that it broke a cable, and I lost my anchor. And here again I was exposed to the mercy of the sea, and the gentleness of an element that could neither distinguish things nor persons. And but that He who stilleth the raging of the sea, and the noise of his waves, and the madness of his people, had provided a plank for me, I had been lost to all the opportunities of content and study. But I know not whether I have been more preserved by the courtesies of my friends, or the gentleness and mercies of a noble enemy." The following passage from the Acts of the Apostles follows in the original Greek. "And the barbarous people showed us no little kindness, for they kindled a fire and received us every one, because of the present rain, and because of the cold."

Bishop Heber traces a parallel between this passage and the circumstances attending Dr. Taylor's capture and imprisonment after the engagement at Cardigan Castle. Mr. Willmott, with we think greater propriety, makes it refer to the general course of the divine's fortunes at this period. He married in Wales, Joanna Bridges, said to have been a natural daughter of King Charles I., when Prince of Wales. Tradition reports the lady to have been very beautiful, and the owner of a large property in Llangadock, in the northeastern part of Caermarthenshire. The estate, Mandinnam, is about two miles from the town. Its revenues had been, probably previous to the marriage, greatly reduced by the exactions of the dominant party, and the unsettled state of public affairs, as we find Dr. Taylor opening a school in this rural district as a means of support. He placed his school in the village of Llanfihangel Aberbythic, and was assisted in its care by William Nicholson, who had been recently ousted by Parliament from a comfortable living in South Wales, and afterwards became Bishop of Gloucester. His other associate, William Wyatt, became a Prebendary of Lincoln. They rented Newton Hall, a house of some importance in the parish, and appear to have been successful in their enterprise. Two of their scholars, Judge Powell, who took a leading part on the trial of the seven Bishops, in the reign of James II., and Griffin Lloyd of Cwmgwilly, were apparently proud of having been educated at the establishment, as their tombstones bear witness to the fact. The school has also left its record in *A New and Easy Institution of Grammar*, a work published in 1647, with a dedicatory epistle in Latin, from the *Collegium Newtoniense*, to Lord Hatton, and another in English from Taylor to Christopher Hatton, the eldest son of the nobleman,—a youth at that time of fifteen, who afterwards became, under Charles the Second, a viscount and governor of the island of Guernsey. The book was probably prepared by Wyatt, as it bears no trace of the more gifted mind of his associate. A pointed remark on the necessity of mental occupation for youth, is one of the few specimens of Dr. Taylor's conversation which have been preserved. "If," he once remarked, "you do not choose to fill your boy's head with something, believe me, the devil will."*

It was probably about this time that Dr. Taylor had his last interview with the monarch whose adverse fortunes he had so faithfully followed. Charles' chaplains were allowed free access to his person, in August, 1647. During Dr. Taylor's visit, at this or a later period, he received from the King, as a testimony of his regard, his watch, and a few pearls and rubies which had ornamented his ebony Bible-case.

In 1647 Dr. Taylor published *The Liberty of Prophesying*, one of the most able of his many valuable works, and enjoying the high honor of having been the first plea in history for toleration and liberty respecting differences of religious belief. Taking the Apostles' Creed as the summary of Christian Doctrine, he regards all differences not embraced in its few and simple sentences as of less import-

* *Seward's Anecdotes*, vol. ii., p. 45; quoted in Bishop Heber's *Life of Taylor*.

ance than the prevalence of peace and harmony.

He then illustrates the difficulties attending the formation of a right judgment on many matters of scriptural belief, not included in this simple and primitive summary, and the inability of tradition, of councils, and of the papal power to determine authoritatively these questions. The solution, if one is needed, must, he holds, be sought by the exercise of our reason. This arbitrator cannot however, any more than those already named, claim infallibility. We are not morally accountable, if, after having used our best endeavors, we arrive at a wrong conclusion; but we are in decided and grievous error, if we attempt to force such decision, whether it be right or wrong, upon our neighbor. "Let not men" he says, "be hasty, in calling every disliked opinion by the name of heresy, and, when they have resolved that they will call it so, let them use the erring person like a brother, not beat him like a dog, nor convince him with a gibbet, or vex him out of his understanding and persuasions."

He then shows, that this tolerant theory is in accordance with the practice of the primitive Church, that it was first used by heretical sects, during their temporary assumption and possession of power; that even after the usurpation of the papacy, life was not exacted as the penalty for holding or teaching doctrines deemed erroneous, until the persecution of the Albigenses.

The civil power is, equally with the ecclesiastical, to extend toleration to diversity of religious opinion, provided that the public peace be not broken by services of a disorderly or immoral nature. The decision, on this point, he leaves to the discretion of the magistrate. He then enters into an examination of the doctrines of the Anabaptists and Roman Catholics, as the two sects "which are most troublesome and most disliked," that "by an account made of these, we may make judgment what may be done towards others, whose errors are not apprehended of so great malignity." After an examination of the doctrines of these sects, including an elaborate examination of the question of infant baptism, and a careful estimate of the extent of these errors, he concludes, that the decision of their toleration is for the magistrate to determine. "Let the prince and the secular power have a care the commonwealth be safe; for whether such or such a sect of Christians be to be permitted, is a question rather political than religious."

Denominations of Christians, agreeing upon topics embraced in the Creed, are, he urges, to commune together. The *Liberty of Prophesying* concludes with one of its author's most beautifully narrated parables. It is not found in the original edition, but was added in that of 1657.

"I end with a story which I find in the Jews' books. When Abraham sat at his tent door, according to his custom, waiting to entertain strangers; he espied an old man stooping and leaning on his staff, weary with age and travel, coming towards him, who was an hundred years of age. He received him kindly, washed his feet, provided supper, caused him to sit down, but observing that the old man eat and prayed not, nor begged for a blessing on his meat, he asked him why he did not worship the God of heaven: the old man told him, that he worshipped the fire only, and acknowledged no other God; at which answer, Abraham grew so zealously angry, that he thrust the old man out of his tent, and exposed him to all the evils of the night and an unguarded condition. When the old man was gone, God called to Abraham, and asked him where the stranger was; he replied, 'I thrust him away, because he did not worship Thee:' God answered him, 'I have suffered him these hundred years, although he dishonored Me, and couldst not thou endure him one night, when he gave thee no trouble.' Upon this, saith the story, Abraham fetched him back again, and gave him hospitable entertainment, and wise instruction. Go thou and do likewise, and thy charity will be rewarded by the God of Abraham."

This story has also been used by Dr. Franklin, in his "Parable of Persecution."

CHAPTER VI.

THE SCHOOL—THE EARL OF CARBERY—GOLDEN GROVE—GRONGAR HILL—THE COUNTESS OF CARBERY—CONTENTMENT—THE LIFE OF CHRIST—THE COUNTESS OF CARBERY'S FUNERAL SERMON.

DR. TAYLOR'S school probably furnished but a moderate addition to his income. He was shielded from want, his works now probably yielding something to their author. He received occasional aid also from a wealthy landed proprietor of the neighborhood, Richard Vaughan, earl of Carbery. This gentleman had distinguished himself as a soldier in the Irish wars, and obtained the Order of the Bath for his good conduct. He had been during the recent conflict the principal royalist commander in South Wales, and was made in consequence, after the Restoration, Lord Vaughan of Emlyn, lord president of Wales, and privy councillor. Though active on the King's side, he seems to have had many friends among the Parliamentarians, so that after the battle of Marston Moor he was able to secure his estates from confiscation. This gentleman lived on his estate of Golden Grove in the parish in which Dr. Taylor now resided. The region, though now deprived to some extent of the fine woods which then graced the landscape, is still celebrated for its romantic beauty. It is watered by the Towy, a stream famed in the far back days of King Arthur and his knights, as the haunt of Merlin, the great enchanter. To the north of Golden Grove, a mile and a half distant, stands Dynevor Castle, the seat of the ancient princes of South Wales, surrounded by venerable oaks. To the west, three miles off, in full view of the house, Dryslwyn Castle surmounts a rocky eminence, as rugged as its name, and Grongar Hill rises on the northwest, a mile and a half from the mansion.

An English poet of some repute, John Dyer, has described the scene in pleasing verse.

"Now I gain the mountain's brow,
What a landscape lies below!
No clouds, no vapors intervene,
But the gay, the open scene
Does the face of Nature show,
In all the hues of heaven's bow!
And, swelling to embrace the light,
Spreads around beyond the sight.

Old castles on the cliffs arise,
Proudly towering in the skies!
Rushing from the woods, the spires
Seem from hence ascending fires;
Half his beams Apollo sheds
On the yellow mountain-heads!
Gilds the fleeces of the flocks;
And glitters on the broken rocks!
Below me trees unnumber'd rise,
Beautiful in various dyes:
The gloomy pine, the poplar blue,
The yellow beech, the sable yew,
The slender fir, that taper grows,
The sturdy oak with broad-spread boughs;
And beyond, the purple grove,
Haunt of Phillis and of love!
Gaudy as the opening dawn,
Lies a long and level lawn,
On which a dark hill, steep and high,
Holds and charms the wand'ring eye!
Deep are his feet in Towy's flood,
His sides are clothed with waving wood,
And ancient towers crown his brow,
That cast an awful look below."

A genial hospitality imparted a charm to the interior of Golden Grove akin to that impressed by Nature on its external features. The mistress of the mansion was one well fitted to dispense its honors. Frances, countess of Carbery, was the daughter of Sir John Altham, of the county of Hertford. Her kindness, with that of her husband, to Dr. Taylor, has secured her an enduring fame from the splendid eulogy which the divine but a few years later pronounced over her grave.

Under these fostering influences of sympathy and friendship, of domestic happiness and the manifold beauties of Nature, Dr. Taylor's mind attained its highest development. It was during the years passed near Golden Grove that he composed and published the works which have conferred upon him his most wide-spread popularity. It was, doubtless, a season of happiness, despite its privations. We can fortunately trace his feelings through several passages in his writings, which, in addition to their autobiographical interest, rank among the most eloquent sentences which his pen ever traced.

"I am fallen," he says in an early chapter of his *Holy Living*, "into the hands of publicans and sequestrators, and they have taken all from me; what now? Let me look about me. They have left me the sun and moon, fire and water, a loving wife, and many friends to pity me, and some to relieve me; and I can still discourse, and, unless I list, they have not taken away my merry countenance, and my cheerful spirit, and a good conscience; they have still left me the providence of God, and all the promises of the Gospel; and my religion, and my hopes of heaven, and my charity to them, too; and still I sleep and digest, I eat and drink, I read and meditate. I can walk in my neighbor's pleasant fields, and see the variety of natural beauties, and delight in all that in which God delights—that is, in virtue and wisdom, in the whole creation, and in God himself. And he that hath so many causes of joy, and so great, is very much in love with sorrow and peevishness, who loses all these pleasures, and chooses to sit down upon his little handful of thorns. Such a person were fit to bear Nero company in his funeral sorrow for the loss of one of Poppæa's hairs, or help to mourn for Lesbia's sparrow; and because he loved it, he deserves to starve in the midst of plenty, and to want comfort while he is encircled with blessings."

Dr. Taylor now published the *Apology for Authorized and Set Forms of Liturgy against the Pretence of the Spirit*, an enlargement of a volume already noticed. It was soon followed by *The Life of Christ, or the Great Exemplar.* This work consists of an amplification of the narratives of the Evangelists, accompanied by reflections upon our Saviour's acts and words, and a number of prayers. He has not entered upon any illustration of the manners and customs of the time, or into any examination of disputed points or passages. He has exercised so little of a critical spirit, as occasionally to introduce, without comment, incidents not found in the New Testament, and resting only upon fanciful legend. His sole object was to produce, so far as his exuberant fancy would permit, a plain, devotional work. "I have chosen," he says in the preface, "to serve the purposes of religion by doing assistance to that part of theology which is wholly practical; that which makes us wiser, therefore, because it makes us better."

The popularity with which this beautiful work was at once greeted, a popularity which it has ever since retained, may have influenced the author in devoting himself, during the three years passed near Golden Grove, to works of a similar character. His splendid eulogy, "A Sermon on the Death of the Excellent Lady Carbery," next followed. This eloquent discourse was delivered at the funeral of the countess, in Llanfihangel Aberbythic church.

We extract a portion of his beautiful tribute to one who appears to have left as wife, mother, and friend, an example of no common brilliancy.

THE COUNTESS OF CARBERY.

I have seen a female religion that wholly dwelt upon the face and tongue; that like a wanton and undressed tree spends all its juice in suckers and irregular branches, in leaves and gum, and after all such goodly outsides, you should never eat an apple, or be delighted with the beauties or the perfumes of a hopeful blossom. But the religion of this excellent lady was of another constitution; it took root downward in humility, and brought forth fruit upward in the substantial graces of a Christian, in charity and justice, in chastity and modesty, in fair friendships and sweetness of society: she had not very much of the forms and outsides of godliness, but she was hugely careful for the power of it, for the moral, essential, and useful parts; such which would make her be, not seem to be, religious.

* * * * * *

In all her religion, in all her actions of relation towards God, she had a strange evenness and untroubled passage, sliding towards her ocean of God and of infinity with a certain and silent motion. So have I seen a river, deep and smooth, passing with a still foot and sober face, and paying to the *fiscus*, the great exchequer of the sea, the prince of all the watery bodies, a tribute large and full: and hard by it a little brook skipping and making a noise upon its unequal and neighbor bottom; and after all its talking and bragged motion, it paid to its common audit no more than the revenues of a little cloud, or a contemptible vessel: so have I sometimes compared the issues of her religion to the solemnities and famed outsides of another's piety. It dwelt upon her spirit, and was incorporated with the periodical work of every day: she did not believe that religion was intended to minister to fame and reputation, but to pardon of sins, to the pleasure of God, and the salvation of souls. For religion is like the breath of heaven; if it goes abroad into the open air, it scatters and dissolves like camphire; but if it enters into a secret hollowness, into a close conveyance, it is strong and mighty, and comes forth with vigor and great effect at the other end, at the other side of this life, in the days of death and judgment.

The other appendage of her religion, which also was a great ornament to all the parts of her life, was a rare modesty and humility of spirit, a confident despising and undervaluing of herself. For though she had the greatest judgment, and the greatest experience of things and persons that I ever yet knew in a person of her youth, and sex, and circumstances; yet, as if she knew nothing of it, she had the meanest opinion of herself; and like a fair taper, when she shined to all the room, yet round about her own station she had cast a shadow and a cloud, and she shined to everybody but herself.

* * * * * *

Her recreations were little and seldom, her prayers often, her reading much: she was of a most noble and charitable soul; a great lover of honorable actions, and as great a despiser of base things; hugely loving to oblige others, and very unwilling to be in arrear to any upon the stock of courtesies and liberality; so free in all acts of favor, that she would not stay to hear herself thanked, as being unwilling that what good went from her to a needful or an obliged person should ever return to her again: she was an excellent friend, and hugely dear to very many, especially to the best and most discerning persons; to all that conversed with her and could understand her great worth and sweetness.

She lived as we all should live, and she died as I fain would die. * * And as now in the grave it shall not be inquired concerning her, how long she lived, but how well, so to us who live after her, to suffer a longer calamity, it may be some ease to our sorrows, and some guide to our lives, and some security to our conditions, to consider that God hath brought the piety of a young lady to the early rewards of a never-ceasing and never-dying eternity of glory: and we also, if we live as she did, shall partake of the same glories; not only having the honor of a good name, and a dear and honored memory, but the glories of these glories, the end of all excellent labors, and all prudent counsels, and all holy religion, even the salvation of our souls, in that day when all the saints, and among them this excellent woman, shall be shown to all the world to have done more, and more excellent things, than we know of, or can describe.

CHAPTER VII.

HOLY LIVING AND DYING—DEATH—SUNRISE—SICKNESS AND SUBMISSION—SERMONS—JOY IN HEAVEN—PRAYER—MARRIAGE—THE TRIUMPH OF CHRISTIANITY—PARENTS.

THE *Rule and Exercise of Holy Living* next appeared. It was followed by a second part, *Holy Dying*, in 1651. The two have always held a prominent place among works designed to aid our conduct in life and prepare us for death. The first part consists of a series of essays on Charity, Justice, and Religion, following out these topics through various subdivisions, and accompanying all by brief counsels and prayers. The second part opens with reflections upon the shortness and uncertainty of life, passing from these it considers the trials and duties incident to sickness and the last hours of life. The style is uniformly eloquent and impressive. Our extracts are taken from the *Holy Dying*.

DEATH.

All the succession of time, all the changes

in nature, all the varieties of light and darkness, the thousand thousands of accidents in the world, and every contingency to every man, and to every creature, doth preach our funeral sermon, and calls us to look and see how the old sexton Time throws up the earth and digs a grave, where we must lay our sins or our sorrows, and sow our bodies till they rise again in a fair or in an intolerable eternity.

* * * * * *

Thus death reigns in all the portions of our time. The Autumn with its fruits provides disorders for us, and the Winter's cold turns them into sharp diseases, and the Spring brings flowers to strew our hearse, and the Summer gives green turf and brambles to bind upon our graves. Calentures and surfeit, cold and agues, are the four quarters of the year, and all minister to Death; and you can go no whither, but you tread upon a dead man's bones.

The wild fellow in Petronius, that escaped upon a broken table from the furies of a shipwreck, as he was sunning himself upon the rocky shore, espied a man rolled upon his floating bed of waves, ballasted with sand in the folds of his garment, and carried by his civil enemy, the sea, towards the shore to find a grave: and it cast him into some sad thoughts; that peradventure this man's wife in some part of the Continent, safe and warm, looks next month for the good man's return; or it may be his son knows nothing of the tempest; or his father thinks of that affectionate kiss which still is warm upon the good old man's cheek ever since he took a kind farewell; and he weeps with joy, to think how blessed he shall be when his beloved boy returns into the circle of his father's arms. These are the thoughts of mortals; this is the end and sum of all their designs: a dark night and an ill guide, a boisterous sea and a broken cable, a hard rock and a rough wind, dashed in pieces the fortune of a whole family; and they that shall weep loudest for the accident, are not yet entered into the storm and yet have suffered shipwreck. Then looking upon the carcass, he knew it, and found it to be the master of the ship, who the day before cast up the accounts of his patrimony and his trade, and named the day when he thought to be at home: see how the man swims who was so angry two days since; his passions are becalmed with the storm, his accounts cast up, his cares at an end, his voyage done, and his gains are the strange events of death, which whether they be good or evil, the men that are alive seldom trouble themselves concerning the interests of the dead.

SUNRISE.

But as when the sun approaches towards the gates of the morning, he first opens a little eye of heaven, and sends away the spirits of darkness, and gives light to a cock, and calls up the lark to matins, and by and by gilds the fringes of a cloud, and peeps over the eastern hills, thrusting out his golden horns, like those which decked the brows of Moses when he was forced to wear a veil, because himself had seen the face of God; and still, while a man tells the story, the sun gets up higher, till he shows a fair face and a full light, and then he shines one whole day, under a cloud often, and sometimes weeping great and little showers, and sets quickly: so is a man's reason and his life.

FITNESS.

No man will hire a general to cut wood, or shake hay with a sceptre, or spend his soul and all his faculties upon the purchase of a cockle-shell; but he will fit instruments to the dignity and exigence of the design.

SICKNESS AND SUBMISSION.

So have I known the boisterous north wind pass through the yielding air, which opened its bosom, and appeased its violence by entertaining it with easy compliance in all the regions of its reception: but when the same breath of Heaven hath been checked with the stiffness of a tower, or the united strength of a wood, it grew mighty, and dwelt there, and made the highest branches stoop, and make a smooth path for it on the top of all its glories. So is sickness and so is the grace of God.

Dr. Taylor's first collection of published sermons, twenty-seven in number, for the summer half-year, was published in 1651. A second volume, containing twenty-five more, for the winter half-year, followed two years after. The collection bears the Greek title *Eniautos.* No order, either of adaptation to the ritual year, or any series of topics appears in the subjects. "The special design of the whole," he states in the Dedication to the Earl of Carbery, "is to describe the greater lines of duty, by special arguments. * * * No man ought to be offended that sermons are not like curious inquiries after new nothings, but pursuances of old truths." The Dedication also states that the sermons "were first presented to God in the ministeries of Lord Carbery's family." The congregation, with the addition of guests, and of the neighboring country people, but a portion of whom it is to be presumed, in a Welsh district, understood English, could not have been large. The sermons are long, several being divided into three and four discourses, and are plentifully sprinkled with quotations in Greek and Latin. They abound in noble bursts of oratory and fine poetical imagery.

We have drawn from the collection of these discourses, in as brief limits as justice to our object would permit, some of their most characteristic passages.

JOY IN HEAVEN.

Every sinner that repents causes joy to Christ, and the joy is so great that it runs over and wets the fair brows and beauteous locks of cherubim and seraphim, and all the angels have a part of that banquet.

Christ's Advent to Judgment.

PRAYER.

Prayer is the peace of our spirit, the stillness of our thoughts, the evenness of recollection, the seat of meditation, the rest of our cares, and the calm of our tempest; prayer is the issue of a quiet mind, of untroubled thoughts, it is the daughter of Charity, and the sister of meekness; and he that prays to God with an angry, that is with a troubled and discomposed spirit, is like him that retires into a battle to meditate, and sets up his closet in the out-quarters of an army, and chooses a frontier garrison to be wise in. Anger is a perfect alienation of the mind from prayer, and therefore is contrary to that attention, which presents our prayers in a right line to God. For so have I seen a lark rising from his bed of grass, and soaring upwards, singing as he rises, and hopes to get to heaven, and climb above the clouds; but the poor bird was beaten back with the loud sighings of an eastern wind, and his motion made irregular and inconstant, descending more at every breath of the tempest, than it could recover by the libration and frequent weighing of his wings; till the little creature was forced to sit down and pant, and stay till the storm was over, and then it made a prosperous flight, and did rise and sing as if it had learned music and motion from an angel, as he passed sometimes through the air about his ministeries here below. So is the prayer of a good man: when his affairs have required business, and his business was matter of discipline, and his discipline was to pass upon a sinning person, or had a design of charity, his duty met with the infirmities of a man, and anger was its instrument, and the instrument became stronger than the prime agent, and raised a tempest and overruled the man; and then his prayer was broken, and his thoughts were troubled, and his words went up towards a cloud, and his thoughts pulled them back again, and made them without intention; and the good man sighs for his infirmity, but must be content to lose the prayer, and he must recover it, when his anger is removed, and his spirit is becalmed, made even as the brow of Jesus, and smooth like the heart of God; and then it ascends to heaven upon the wings of the holy dove, and dwells with God, till it returns like the useful bee, loaden with a blessing and the dew of heaven. *The Return of Prayers.*

MARRIAGE.

Here is the proper scene of piety, and patience, of the duty of parents, and the charity of relatives; here kindness is spread abroad, and love is united and made firm as a centre. Marriage is the nursery of heaven: the virgin sends prayers to God, but she carries but one soul to him; but the state of marriage fills up the numbers of the elect, and hath in it the labor of love, and the delicacies of friendship, the blessing of society, and the union of hands and hearts; it hath in it less of beauty, but more of safety, than the single life; it hath more care but less danger; it is more merry, and more sad; it is fuller of sorrows, and fuller of joys; it lies under more burdens, but is supported by all the strengths of love and charity, and those burdens are delightful. Marriage is the mother of the world, and preserves kingdoms, and fills cities, and churches, and heaven itself. Celibate, like the fly in the heart of an apple, dwells in a perpetual sweetness, but sits alone, and is confounded, and dies in singularity; but marriage, like the useful bee, builds a house and gathers sweetness from every flower, and labors, and unites into societies and republics, and sends out colonies, and feeds the world with delicacies, and obeys their King, and keeps order, and exercises many virtues, and promotes the interest of mankind, and is that state of good things, to which God hath designated the present constitution of the world.

* * * * * * *

Every little thing can blast an infant blossom; and the breath of the south can shake the little rings of the vine, when first they begin to curl, like the locks of a new weaned boy; but when, by age and consolidation, they stiffen into the hardness of a stem, and have, by the warm embraces of the sun and the kisses of heaven, brought forth their clusters, they can endure the storms of the north, and the loud voices of a tempest, and yet never be broken: so are the early unions of an unfixed marriage; watchful and observant, jealous and busy, inquisitive and careful, and apt to take alarm at every unkind word.

The Marriage Ring.

THE TRIUMPH OF CHRISTIANITY.

They that had overcome the world could not strangle Christianity. But so have I seen the sun, with a little ray of distant light, challenge all the power of darkness; and, without violence and noise climbing up the hill, hath made night so to retire, that its memory was lost in the joys and sprightfulness of the morning. And Christianity,—without violence or armies, without resistance and self-preservation, without strength or human eloquence, without challenging of privileges or fighting against tyranny, without alteration of government and scandal of princes, with its humility and meekness, with toleration and patience, with obedience and charity, with praying and dying,—did insensibly turn the world into Christian, and persecution into victory.

The Faith and Patience of the Saints.

PARENTS.

In parents and their children, there is so great a society of nature and of manners, of blessing and cursing, that an evil parent cannot perish in a single death: and holy parents never eat their meal of blessing alone, but they make the room shine like the fire of holy sacrifice; and a father's or a mother's piety makes all the house festival, and full of joy, from generation to generation.

The Entail of Curses cut off.

CHAPTER VIII.

THE REAL PRESENCE—DR. WARNER—GOLDEN GROVE—HYMNS — ADVENT — CHARITY — STATE OF RELIGION—IMPRISONMENT—JOHN EVELYN—UNUM NECESSARIUM—ORIGINAL SIN—DR. WARNER—AGAIN IMPRISONED—DISLIKE TO CONTROVERSY.

IN 1654, roused by the triumphant exultations of some Roman Catholic writers over the low condition of the Church of England, Dr. Taylor again engaged in controversial theology, and published the *Real Presence and Spiritual of Christ in the Blessed Sacrament, proved against the Doctrine of Transubstantiation.* It was dedicated to Dr. Warner, bishop of Rochester, who appears to have spared from his scanty means, during the season of deprivation, towards the support of the author.

In 1655, Dr. Taylor expanded a brief catechism, which he had some time before prepared, into a manual of instruction and devotion, called, in graceful compliment to his pleasant shelter, *The Golden Grove:* this little work is divided into Credenda, or what is to be believed, including a catechism and exposition of the Creed; Agenda, or things to be done, a collection of rules for daily, spiritual guidance; Postulanda, or things to be prayed for, a paraphrase of the Lord's Prayer, a Litany, and daily devotions. These are followed by *Festival Hymns*, the only poetical compositions in the entire range of the author's works. The hymns are twenty-two in number. They are irregular in versification, involved in style, and, after the fashion of the time, abound in conceits. The cultivated taste of Bishop Heber, however, pronounces them, after alluding to these apparent faults, "powerful, affecting, and often harmonious:" with "passages of which Cowley need not have been ashamed; and some which remind us, not disadvantageously, of the corresponding productions of Milton."

We present two of these compositions.

THE SECOND HYMN FOR ADVENT;

OR, CHRIST'S COMING TO JERUSALEM IN TRIUMPH.

Lord, come away;
Why dost thou stay?
Thy road is ready; and thy paths, made straight,
With longing expectation wait
The consecration of thy beauteous feet.
Ride on triumphantly; behold, we lay
Our lusts and proud wills in thy way.
Hosannah! welcome to our hearts; Lord, here
Thou hast a temple, too, and full as dear
As that of Sion; and as full of sin;—
Nothing but thieves and robbers dwell therein.
Enter, and chase them forth, and cleanse the floor,
Crucify them, that they may never more
Profane that holy place,
Where thou hast chose to set thy face.
And then if our stiff tongues shall be
Mute in the praises of thy deity,
The stones out of the temple wall
Shall cry aloud and call
Hosannah! and thy glorious footsteps greet. Amen.

A PRAYER FOR CHARITY.

Full of mercy, full of love,
Look upon us from above;
Thou, who taught'st the blind man's night
To entertain a double light,
Thine and the day's (and that thine, too);
The lame away his crutches threw;
The parchèd crust of leprosy
Return'd unto its infancy;

The dumb amazèd was to hear
His own unchain'd tongue strike his ear;
Thy powerful mercy did even chase
The devil from his usurp'd place,
Where thou thyself shouldst dwell, not he.
Oh, let thy love our pattern be;
Let thy mercy teach one brother
To forgive and love another;
That, copying thy mercy here,
Thy goodness may hereafter rear
Our souls unto thy glory, when
Our dust shall cease to be with men. Amen.

In the address "To the Pious and Devout Reader," the author contrasts the condition of religion in England under Episcopacy, with that of his date of writing, much to the disadvantage of the latter. "The people are," he says, "fallen under the harrows and saws of impertinent and ignorant preachers, who think all religion is a sermon, and all sermons ought to be libels against truth and old governors,—and expound chapters that the meaning may never be understood,—and pray, that they may be thought able to talk, but not to hold their peace,—casting not to obtain any thing but wealth and victory, power and plunder. And the people have reaped the fruits apt to grow upon such crabstocks; they grow idle and false, hypocrites and careless; they deny themselves nothing that is pleasant; they despise religion, forget government, and some never think of heaven; and they that do, think to go thither in such paths which all the ages of the Church did give men warning of, lest they should, that way, go to the devil."

For this, with other like vigorous free speech, Dr. Taylor was imprisoned. His confinement does not appear to have been a long one.

On the sixteenth of April, 1654, John Evelyn records in his diary that he heard Dr. Taylor preach in London. Mr. Evelyn was a gentleman of education and fortune who had recently returned from an extensive foreign tour. Although an earnest royalist, his conduct had been so prudent, and his character was so respected, that he lived unmolested by the now dominant party. On the eighteenth of March, we find Mr. Evelyn again one of Dr. Taylor's congregation; and, on the thirty-first of the same month, visiting him "to confer with him about some spiritual matters, using him thenceforward as his ghostly father." Mr. Evelyn continued to be Dr. Taylor's firm friend during the troubles of the Commonwealth, and the remainder of his career,—often aiding him liberally from his private fortune.

Dr. Taylor's next work, "*Unum Necessarium*, or the Doctrine and Practice of Repentance; describing the Necessity and Measures of a Strict, a Holy, and a Christian Life, and Rescued from Popular Errors," involved him in controversy by his denial, in the course of the volume, that mankind were subject to condemnation on account of their original sin derived from Adam.

It must be admitted that Dr. Taylor's views upon this subject were erroneous. In his anxiety to avoid a belief which he charges upon the Calvinists of that day, declaring the condition of infants dying unbaptized to be hopeless, he has fallen into an opposite error in asserting that our inheritance from Adam is one of temporal evil only. According to his theory, a human being now enters the world as Adam did, pure and sinless. Our first parent, he affirms, had supernatural aids afforded him, by which he maintained his innocence until his disobedience and fall, when these aids were withdrawn, nor have they been vouchsafed to his posterity.

It seems strange that an intellect so powerful as Dr. Taylor's did not perceive that this theory affords no solution to the difficulty. The loss of this "supernatural aid" was certainly the same in effect to Adam and his posterity as his fall from innocence. It is but a repetition, in a complicated form, of the simple old adage, that

In Adam's fall
We sinned all.

The remainder of the work is in harmony with the general tone of his writings, of a simple, practical character, enforcing the necessity of repentance, and dwelling with his wonted warmth on the beauty of holiness. The various chapters close with prayers in harmony with their subject-matter, and the general tenor of the whole neutralizes any evil effects which his speculations might occasion. No one ever held more humble views of himself, or of his fellow-men, than Jeremy Taylor. No one has more earnestly confessed the need of the Atonement, or expressed a more fervent gratitude for that greatest of blessings, than he has impressed upon his writings. His eagerness "to vindicate the ways of God to man," proceeded from his ardent piety; but like many examples of similar eagerness, led him beyond the sober limits of reverence and common-sense. We are placed in this world to struggle with sin, not to discuss its origin.

The preface to the *Doctrine of Repentance* is addressed to the Bishops of Salisbury and Rochester. The prelates could not allow doctrines at variance with those of the Articles of the Church to pass unrebuked. The Bishop of Rochester, Dr. Warner, addressed a letter to the author on the subject.

It was dated July 28th, but was not received until September the 11th. The delay was owing to a second imprisonment, which Dr. Taylor was now undergoing, in Chepstow Castle, in consequence of a royalist insurrection at Salisbury, which, although he took no part in the affair, rendered him an object of suspicion. In his reply to the Bishop he explains this delay, adding a passage which throws some light upon his condition. "I have now," he says, "that liberty that I can receive any letters, and send any; for the gentlemen under whose custody I am, as they are careful of their charges, so they are civil to my person." A second letter, in which he requests the Bishop to revise a *Further Expli-*

cation of the Doctrine of Original Sin, a tract prepared by him during his imprisonment, in reply to his theological opponents, dated Mandinam, November 17, 1655, shows that his confinement was of brief duration. He expresses the hope that this second treatise may so explain the first as to "give satisfaction to the Church and to my jealous brethren;" and enters into an elaborate examination of the Ninth Article, in an endeavor to show that his doctrines were not in conflict with its declarations. The Bishop was unconvinced, and refused to revise the tract, which soon after appeared in a second edition of the original publication. It now forms the seventh chapter of the work.

In this letter Dr. Taylor also expresses a desire to avoid controversy, that he may devote his entire attention to a great work upon which he was engaged. "I am very desirous to be permitted quietly to continue my studies," he writes, "that I may seasonably publish the first three books of my *Cases of Conscience*, which I am now preparing for the press, and by which, as I hope to serve God and the Church, so I do design to do some honor to your lordship, to whose charity and nobleness I and my relatives are so much obliged."

In a letter dated November 21, he alludes with some natural feeling to the reception of his *Unum Necessarium*. "I am well pleased that you have read over my last book; and give God thanks that I have reason to believe that it is accepted by God, and by some good men. As for the censure of unconsenting persons, I expected it, and hope that themselves will be their own reprover, and truth will be assisted by God, and shall prevail, when all noises and prejudices shall be ashamed. My comfort is, that I have the honor to be an advocate for God's justice and goodness, and that the consequent of my doctrine is, that men may speak honor of God, and meanly of themselves. But I have also this last week sent up some papers, in which I make it appear that the doctrine which I now have published was taught by the fathers within the first four hundred years; and have vindicated it both from novelty and singularity. I have also prepared some other papers concerning this question, which I once had some thoughts to have published. But what I have already said, and now further explicated and justified, I hope may be sufficient to satisfy pious and prudent persons, who do not love to go *quà itur*, but *quà eundum est.*"*

This letter shows that its writer had devoted earnest thought and study to the subject upon which he had written, and had convinced himself that he was in the right. It also displays his willingness to forbear further discussion, in his love for the peace and quiet of the Church.

* Not the way men go, but the way they should go.

CHAPTER IX.

WANTS OF CHURCHMEN—LETTERS TO MR. EVELYN—PERSECUTION—VISIT TO LONDON—BERKELEY, BOYLE, AND WILKINS—SAY'S COURT—ENJOYMENT OF PROSPERITY—MONSIEUR LE FRANC—A POOR BISHOP—MR. THURLAND—RESIDENCE IN LONDON—DEATH OF A CHILD—SACRED POETRY—DIES IRÆ—DOMESTIC AFFLICTION.

WE find, from a letter by Dr. Taylor, that his friend Mr. Evelyn had urged him to prepare some work adapted to the wants of Episcopalians during their deprivation of public worship and sacraments, under the stern rule of Cromwell. The reply is eminently devout and judicious.

"Dear Sir," he writes, "I perceive by your symptoms how the spirits of pious men are affected in this sad catalysis: it is an evil time, and we ought not to hold our peace; but now the question is,—who shall speak? Yet I am highly persuaded, that, to good men and wise, a persecution is nothing but the changing the circumstances of religion, and the manner of the forms and appendages of divine worship. Public or private is all one: the first hath the advantage of society, the second of love. There is a warmth and light in that, there is a heat and zeal in this; and if every person that can, will but consider concerning the essentials of religion, and retain them severally, and immure them as well as he can with the same or equivalent ceremonies, I know no difference in the thing, but that he shall have the exercise, and, consequently, the reward of other graces, for which, if he lives and dies in prosperous days, he shall never be crowned. But the evils are, that some will be tempted to quit their present religion, and some to take a worse, and some to take none at all. It is a true and sad story; but *oportet esse hœreses*, for so they that are faithful shall be known; and I am sure He that hath promised to bring good out of evil, and that all things shall co-operate to the good of them that fear God, will verify it concerning persecution."

He replies to an invitation to the metropolis: "Sir, I know not when I shall be able to come to London; for our being stripped of the little relics of our fortune remaining after the shipwreck, leaves not cordage nor sails sufficient to bear me thither. But I hope to be able to commit to the press my first books of *Conscience* by Easter time; and then, if I be able to get up, I shall be glad to wait upon you; of whose good I am not more solicitous than I am joyful that you so carefully provide for it in your best interest."

Dr. Taylor appears to have been soon after in a better financial position than he anticipated, as we find him visiting London, and on the 12th of April dining with Mr. Evelyn at his country-seat of Say's Court, near the city. The guests were eminent men, Berkeley, Boyle, and Wilkins. Berkeley, to whom the severe and critical pen of Pope has assigned "every virtue under heaven," was then earning his claim to the gratitude of both hemispheres by his efforts to obtain the endowment of his college in the Bermudas.

Robert Boyle was one of the most accomplished scholars and devout churchmen of his day.*

"Wilkins," says Mr. Willmott, "was a person of singular ingenuity, and deserves to be remembered as one of the earliest English schol-

---

* *Life of Bishop Ken.*

ars who endeavored to make science popular and practical. His fancy, however, outran his judgment. His theory of a passage to the moon, provoked the smile of his contemporaries, and subsequently caught the eye of Pope—

> 'The head that turns at superlunar things,
> Poised on a tail, may steer on Wilkins' wings.'

"His retort to the Duchess of Newcastle would alone have authorized a claim to conversational eminence. 'Where,' inquired the rhyming lady, 'am I to find a place to bait, if I try the journey to that planet?' 'Madam,' replied the discoverer, 'of all the people in the world, I least expected that question from you, who have built so many castles in the air, that you may lie every night in one of your own.' Wilkins appeals to our sympathy upon stronger ground than his science or wit would furnish. Related to Cromwell by a marriage with his sister, he employed his influence on behalf of persecuted piety and learning, and the preservation of the universities has been attributed to his energetic remonstrances."*

---

* *Life of Taylor*, p. 154.

Four days later the divine addressed the following letter of thanks and advice to his entertainer. It is wise, dignified, and affectionate, the solemn duties of the clergyman tempering the admiration of the scholar. Mr. Evelyn was one of the most celebrated *virtuosi* of his time. He had collected during his long tour a variety of interesting objects, and was constantly adding to their number.

April 16, 1656.

"HONORED AND DEAR SIR:

"I hope your servant brought my apology with him, and that I already am pardoned, or excused in your thoughts, that I did not return an answer yesterday to your friendly letter. Sir, I did believe myself so very much bound to you for your so kind, so friendly reception of me in your *Tusculanum*, that I had some little wonder upon me when I saw you making excuses that it was no better. Sir, I came to see you and your lady, and am highly pleased that I did so, and found all your circumstances to be a heap and union of blessings. But I have not either so great a fancy and opinion of the prettiness of your abode, or so low an opinion of your prudence and piety, as to think you can be any ways transported with them. I know the pleasure of them is gone off from their height before one month's possession; and that strangers, and seldom seers, feel the beauty of them more than you who dwell with them. I am pleased indeed at the order and cleanness of all your outward things; and look upon you not only as a person, by way of thankfulness to God for his mercies and goodness to you, specially obliged to a great measure of piety, but also as one who, being freed in great degree from secular cares and impediments, can, without excuse and allay, wholly intend what you so passionately desire, the service of God. But, now I am considering yours, and enumerating my own pleasures, I cannot but add, that, though I could not choose but be delighted by seeing all about you, yet my delices were really in seeing you severe and unconcerned in these things, and now in finding your affections wholly a stranger to them, and to communicate with them no portion of your passion but such as is necessary to him that uses them or receives their ministries."

A few days after, on the 6th of May, Mr. Evelyn records in his diary, bringing "Monsieur le Franc, a young French Sorbonist"* to converse with Dr. Taylor. On the following day he prevailed on the Doctor, who had been much pleased with the young man, to present him to the Bishop. The candidate was ordained deacon and priest on the same day by a prelate whom Mr. Evelyn calls the Bishop of Meath. As that see was vacant from the death of the last incumbent, Dr. Anthony Martin, until after the Restoration, he is doubtless in error in respect to the title. He mentions that he "paid the fees to his lordship, who was very poor and in great want. To that necessity were our clergy reduced!"

Dr. Taylor remained but a short time in London, as we find him, on the 19th of July, writing from Wales to his friend Mr. Evelyn. The latter appears to have communicated an offer from Mr. Edward Thurland to furnish him with an asylum in London. Mr., afterwards Sir Edward Thurland, and one of the barons of the Exchequer, was a celebrated lawyer, and author of a work on Prayer, highly commended by Mr. Evelyn in a letter to the

* A student of the celebrated college, the Sorbonne, in Paris.

writer, after a perusal of the manuscript. In this letter, Dr. Taylor confesses that he looks with a student's wistful eye to the metropolis. "Truly, sir," he says, "I do continue in my desires to settle about London, and am only hindered by my *res angusta domi;* but hope in God's goodness that he will create to me such advantages as may make it possible; and when I am there, I shall expect the daily issues of the Divine Providence to make all things else well, because I am much persuaded that, by my abode in the voisinage of London, I may receive advantages of society and books to enable me better to serve God and the interest of souls. I have no other design but it, and I hope God will second it with his blessing. Sir, I desire you to present my thanks and service to Mr. Thurland; his society were argument enough to make me desire a dwelling thereabouts, but his other kindnesses will make it possible. I would not be troublesome, serviceable I would fain be, useful, and desirable; and I will endeavor it, if I come."

The letter closes with a beautiful passage in allusion to a recent domestic bereavement.

"Dear Sir, I am in some little disorder by reason of the death of a little child of mine, a boy that lately made us very glad; but now he rejoices in his little orb, while we think, and sigh, and long to be as safe as he is."

In another letter he expresses a wish, often felt by many friends of the English Church. After congratulating his friend Evelyn upon his translation of Lucretius, then just published, he continues: "It is a thousand pities but our English tongue should be enriched with a translation of all the sacred hymns which are respersed in all the rituals and church books. I was thinking to have begged of you a translation of that well-known hymn, '*Dies iræ, dies illa, solvet seclum in favilla*,' which, if it were a little changed, would be an excellent divine song; but I am not willing to bring trouble to you: only it is a thousand times to be lamented that the *beaux esprits* of England do not think divine things to be worthy subjects for their poesy and spare hours."

The "*beaux esprits*" were less in fault than the writer charges. Some of the most beautiful sacred poetry in the English language was written by his contemporaries or immediate predecessors; and it was but a few years before, that the fine hymn he mentions had been translated, with a success not surpassed by many subsequent efforts, by the poet Crashaw. The expression of this desire from the acknowledged master of poetical imagery and melody in devotional prose, deserves to rank among the most interesting and curious coincidences in the history of literature, when we remember that the composition of *Paradise Lost* is supposed to have been commenced in the same year.*

Mr. Evelyn seems to have determined to follow out his friend's suggestion, as we find Dr. Taylor remarking, in a letter dated "9ber. 1656. I am very desirous to receive the '*dies iræ, dies illa*,' of your translation; and if you have not yet found it, upon notice of it from you, I will transmit a copy of it."

Dr. Taylor's house was soon again saddened by the loss of two of his remaining children by his second marriage. His letter, announcing the event, has no address, but is supposed from its affectionate tone to have been sent to Mr. Evelyn.

"I have passed through a great cloud which hath wetted me deeper than the skin. It hath pleased God to send the small-pox and fevers

* Willmott's *Life of Taylor*, p. 160.

among my children; and I have, since I received your last, buried two sweet, hopeful boys; and have now but one son left, whom I intend, if it please God, to bring up to London before Easter, and then I hope to wait upon you, and by your sweet conversation and other divertisements, if not to alleviate my sorrow, yet, at least, to entertain myself and keep me from too intense and actual thinkings of my trouble. * * * * * *
For myself, I bless God I have observed and felt so much mercy in this angry dispensation of God, that I am almost transported, I am sure, highly pleased, with thinking how infinitely sweet his mercies are, when his judgments are so gracious. Sir, there are many particulars in your letter which I would fain have answered; but, still, my little sadnesses intervene, and will yet suffer me to write nothing else, but that I beg your prayers, and that you will still own me to be, dear and honored sir, your very affectionate friend, and hearty servant,

"JER. TAYLOR.

"*Feb.* 22, 1656–7."

It is remarkable that the writer speaks of "but one son left," when we know by other evidence that two other sons, by his first wife, both lived to manhood. It is probable that these now resided with their mother's relatives, and that Dr. Taylor alluded only to the family gathered under his own roof.

CHAPTER X.

REMOVAL TO LONDON—DEUS JUSTIFICATU—GAULE AND JEANES—CONTROVERSY—MR. EVELYN'S BENEVOLENCE—DR. TAYLOR'S ACKNOWLEDGMENT—COLLECTION OF WORKS—TREATISE ON FRIENDSHIP—MRS. PHILLIPS—DR. WEDDERBURNE—EPISCOPACY IN LONDON—BISHOP PEARSON—IMPRISONMENT—CONDOLENCE.

THE tradition of the neighborhood coincides with the statement of the Oxford biographer, Anthony Wood, that Dr. Taylor left Wales in consequence of his domestic bereavements, and removed to London, where he officiated privately for a small congregation of Episcopalians. His mind was harassed at this period of sorrow by controversy. He had published, in 1656, "*Deus Justificatus;* or, A Vindication of the Glory of the Divine Attributes, in the Question of Original Sin," accompanied by the "Explication" already mentioned, dedicated to Bishop Warner. In this he reiterated his opinions on the subject of original sin. He was called to account for these by two Puritan clergymen, John Gaule, of Staughton, Huntingdonshire, who published a work entitled *Sapientia Justificata*, which Dr. Taylor never noticed, and Henry Jeanes, minister of Chedzoy in Somersetshire. He was drawn into a correspondence with the latter, through a common friend, and became gradually so excited as to lose his temper. Mr. Jeanes published this correspondence, and afterwards returned to the charge in a treatise, published in 1660, to which Dr. Taylor made no reply. The adversary conducted his case with ability. He had been a contemporary of Dr. Taylor at Oxford, where he was celebrated for his opposition to the Puritans. In 1641, we find him active on the opposite side. He maintained throughout, a reputation for learning, ability, and moderation to his opponents. In his account of the origin of the controversy, he pays a high tribute to the abilities of his distinguished antagonist. In his "advertisement to the unprejudiced reader," he speaks as follows.

"One Mr. T. C. [Thomas Cartwright], of Bridgewater, being at my house, brake out into extraordinary (that I say not excessive and hyperbolical) praises of Dr. Jeremy Taylor. I expressed my concurrence with him in great part, nay, I came nothing behind him, in the just commendations of his admirable wit, great parts, quick and elegant pen, his abilities in critical learning, and his profound skill in antiquity."

We gladly pass from the angry arena of controversy, to the calmer and purer atmosphere surrounding friendly intercourse, and the interchange of good works. Mr. Evelyn, with the fellow-feeling of a scholar, seems to have been keenly alive to his friend's pecuniary annoyances. He not only gave liberally himself, but called out like assistance from his brothers. He wrote on the 9th of May, as follows. "Among the rest that are tributaries to your worth, I make bold to present you with this small token, and though it bears no proportion, either with my obligation, or your merit, yet I hope you will accept it as the product of what I have employed for this purpose; and which you shall yearly receive, so long as God makes me able, and that it may be useful. What I can handsomely do for you, by other friends, as occasions present themselves, may, I hope, in time supply that which I myself would do. In order to which, I have already made one of my brothers sensible of this opportunity, to do God and his Church an acceptable service. I think I shall prevail as much on the other."

The delicately worded offer met with a fitting response from the grateful recipient.

"HONORED AND DEAR SIR:—A stranger came two nights since from you, with a letter and a token; full of humanity and sweetness that was, and this of charity. I know it is more blessed to give than to receive; and as I no ways repine at the Providence that forces me to receive, so neither can I envy that felicity of yours, not only that you can, but that you do give; and as I rejoice in that mercy which daily makes decree in heaven for my support and comfort, so I do most thankfully adore the goodness of God to you, whom he consigns to greater glories, by the ministeries of these graces. But, sir, what am I, or what can I do, or what have I done, that you think I have or can oblige you? Sir, you are too kind to me, and oblige me not only beyond my merit, but beyond my modesty. I only can love you, and honor you, and pray for you: and in all this, I cannot say but that I am behindhand with you, for I have found so great effluxes of all your worthiness and charities, that I am a debtor for your prayers, for the comfort of your letters, for the charity of your hand, and the affections of your heart. Sir, though you are beyond the reach of my returns, and my services are very short of touching you, yet if it were possible for me to receive any commands, the obeying of which might signify my great regards of you, I could with some more confidence converse with a person so obliging; but I am obliged, and ashamed, and unable to say so much as I should do to represent myself to be, honored and dear sir, your most affectionate and obliged friend and servant,

JER. TAYLOR.

May, 15, 1657.

In 1657, a collection of several of Dr. Taylor's works appeared in a folio volume, with the title, *Sumbolon Ethico Polemicon; or, a Collection of Polemical and Moral Discourses.* It contained the "Liberty of Prophesying" (to which he now added the beautiful parable of Abraham, already quoted in these pages), the "Golden Grove," the "Apology for authorized and set forms of Liturgy," and other treatises already in print; but with these were included, the "Treatise on Friendship," and "Two Letters to persons changed in their religion," which were now first made perfect.

The Treatise on Friendship, one of his most beautiful productions, is dedicated to Mrs. Katherine Phillips. This lady was the wife of James Phillips, Esq., of the Priory at Cardigan. She was a great favorite with the authors of the day, claiming herself membership of the guild by a number of occasional poems, which were published in a folio volume after her death, and was frequently complimented under the title of the "Matchless Orinda," a name she had assumed in conducting a long correspondence with a friend, Sir Charles Cotterel. Her poetry is smoothly written, but does not take any elevated rank. She was a lady of exemplary character and great amiability, qualities which, combined with a handsome person and easy fortune, will go far in accounting for her popularity.

The dedication to the Matchless Orinda, is not the only tribute of a personal character which graces this Treatise on Friendship. We find, from a postscript addressed to the same lady that the work itself was due to the inspiration of the noble virtue it so eloquently commemorates, having been written for the private perusal of his friends, without any design of publication. He alluded to one of these friends, his physician, Dr. Wedderburne, with tender affection and graceful eulogy. "If you shall think fit that these papers pass further than your own eye and closet, I desire they may be consigned into the hands of my worthy friend, Dr. Wedderburne; for I do not only expose all my sickness to his cure, but I submit my weaknesses to his censure, being as confident to find of him charity for what is pardonable, as remedy for what is curable: but, indeed, madam, I look upon that worthy man as an *idea* of friendship, and if I had no other notices of friendship or conversation, to instruct me than his, it were sufficient; for whatsoever I can say of friendship, I can say of his, and as all that know him, reckon him among the best physicians, so I know him worthy to be reckoned among the best friends."

Dr. Wedderburne was one of the physicians in ordinary to Charles the First. He was originally a professor of philosophy at St. Andrew's, afterwards travelled, and, says Anthony Wood, "became so celebrated for his great skill in physic, that he was the chief man of this country for many years for that faculty. Afterwards he received the honor of knighthood, and was highly valued when he was in Holland with the Prince in 1646–7. At length, though his infirmities and great age forced him to retire from public practice and business, yet his fame contracts * all the Scotch nation to him, and his noble hospitality, and kindness to all that were learned and virtuous, made his conversation no less loved than his advice was desired." †

It is difficult to decide whether Dr. Taylor was at this time permanently residing in, or only a frequent visitor to the metropolis. Anthony Wood states that he left Wales and took charge of a small congregation in London. The use of the Liturgy had been forbidden by law some years previously, but a Puritan regulation, established in 1641, whereby every parish was authorized to found and maintain a lecture, was now turned to the service of the Church it was designed to molest, as several congregations, deprived of their

---

* A curious example of the use of the word in the sense of "draws together."

† Bishop Heber's *Life of Taylor*.

lawful rectors, employed lecturers known to belong to the episcopal and monarchical party. The jurisdiction of the Triers, the celebrated functionaries to whom the examination of church affairs was committed, being limited to parishes supported by tithes, they could not touch the lecturers who depended upon what is now known as the voluntary system. A few clergymen of the Church thus continued to preach during the period of the Commonwealth: one of the number was Bishop Pearson, of Chester, who delivered his celebrated lectures on the Creed, in St. Clement's, Eastcheap, in 1659. If Dr. Taylor did not accept any ministerial charge, we have evidence, in the diary of Mr. Evelyn, that he once, at least, officiated in London at this period.

We next hear of Dr. Taylor as again a prisoner. His publisher, Royston, had prefixed to his "Collection of Offices," an engraving of our Saviour, kneeling. All representations of sacred objects were at this time condemned as popish. This superstitious dread of superstition had caused great losses to the nation, by the destruction of painted windows, and statues in the churches, the dispersion of the late King's picture-gallery and other collections.

The engraving was probably only taken notice of as a means of annoyance, Mr. Evelyn expressly stating, in his diary, that the prosecution was owing to the printer having offended the Lieutenant of the Tower. Through the influence of Dr. Taylor's ever-constant friend with this functionary, to whose charge the divine had been committed, the printer having escaped arrest, the prisoner was soon set at liberty.

We have read Dr. Taylor's letter to Mr. Evelyn, in which he "opened his grief" on the the loss of his sons. It was now his province to comfort the same friend under a similar bereavement. He writes to him from his prison:

Dear Sir:—

If dividing and sharing griefs were like the cutting of rivers, I dare say to you, you would find your stream much abated; for I account myself to have a great cause of sorrow, not only in the diminution of your joys and hopes, but in the loss of that pretty person, your strangely hopeful boy. I cannot tell all my own sorrows without adding to yours; and the causes of my real sadness in your loss are so just, and so reasonable, that I can no otherwise comfort you, but by telling you, that you have very great cause to mourn. So certain it is that grief does propagate as fire does. You have enkindled my funeral torch, and by joining mine to yours, I do but increase the flame. '*Hoc me male urit*,' is the best signification of my apprehension of your sad story. But, sir, I cannot choose, but I must hold another, and a brighter flame to you: it is already burning in your heart; and if I can but remove the dark side of the lantern, you have enough within you to warm yourself and to shine to others. Remember, sir, your two boys are two bright stars, and their innocence is secured, and you shall never hear evil of them again. Their state is safe, and heaven is given to them upon very easy terms; nothing but to be born and die. It will cost you more trouble to get where they are; and among other things, one of the hardnesses will be, that you must overcome even this just and reasonable grief; and, indeed, though the grief hath but too reasonable a cause, yet it is much more reasonable that you master it. For besides that they are no losers, but you are the person that complains, do but consider what you would have suffered for their interest: you would have suffered them to go from you, to be great princes in a strange country, and if you can be content to suffer your own inconvenience for their interest, you command [commend] your worthiest love, and the question of mourning is at an end. But you have said, and done well, when you look upon it as a rod of God; and he that so smites here, will spare hereafter: and if you, by patience and submission, imprint the discipline upon your own flesh, you kill the cause, and make the effect very tolerable; because it is, in some sense, chosen, and, therefore, in no sense insufferable. Sir, if you do not look to it, time will snatch your honor from you, and reproach you for not effecting that by Christian philosophy, which time will do alone. And if you consider, that of the bravest men in the world we find the seldomest stories of their children, and the Apostles had none, and thousands of the worthiest persons, that sound most in story, died childless, you will find it is a rare act of Providence, so to impose upon worthy men a necessity of perpetuating their names by worthy actions and discourses, governments, and reasonings. If the breach be never repaired, it is because God does not see it fit to be; and if you will be of this mind, it will be much the better. But, sir, you will pardon my zeal and passion for your comfort: I will readily confess that you have no need of any discourse from me to comfort you. Sir, now you have an opportunity of serving God by passive graces; strive to be an example and a comfort to your lady, and by your wise counsel and comfort, stand in the breaches of your own family, and make it appear that you are more to her than ten sons. Sir, by the assistance of Almighty God, I purpose to wait on you some time next week, that I may be a witness of your Christian courage and bravery, and that I may see that God never displeases you, as long as the main stake is preserved—I mean your hopes and confidences of heaven. Sir, I shall pray for all that you can want—that is, some degrees of comfort, and a present mind; and shall always do you honor, and fain also would do you service, if it were in the power, as it is in the affections and desires of

Dear Sir, your most affectionate and
obliged friend and servant,
JER. TAYLOR.

Feb. 17, 1657-8.

An entry in Mr. Evelyn's diary, eight days later, shows Dr. Taylor happily at liberty to keep his promise.—"Feb. 25. Came Dr. Jeremy Taylor and my brothers, with other friends, to visit and condole with us."

We find a little further on in the same record, that on the 7th of March, Mr. Evelyn went to London "to hear Dr. Taylor in a private house on Luke xiii. 23, 24. After the sermon followed the blessed communion, of which I participated. In the afternoon Dr. Gunning, of Excester House, expounding part of the Creed."

CHAPTER XI.

LECTURESHIP — LETTERS TO MR. EVELYN — RELIGION — INTEREST—DR. PETTY—LORD CONWAY—PORTMORE—LOUGHS NEAGH AND BAG—RAM ISLAND—LITERARY NEWS—TANDY—ACKNOWLEDGMENTS TO MR. EVELYN.

AN offer seems to have been made soon after this, through Mr. Evelyn, by Edward, earl of Conway, to Dr. Taylor, of a lectureship in the vicinity of Lisburn, Ireland. It is alluded to in the following letter, which possesses an interest from its picture of parochial affairs under the Commonwealth.

To John Evelyn, Esquire.

May 12, 1658.

Honored Sir:—I return you many thanks for your care of my temporal affairs: I wish I may be able to give you as good account of my watchfulness for your service, as you have of your diligence to do me benefit. But concerning the thing itself, I am to give you this account. I like not the condition of being a lecturer under the dispose of another, nor to serve in my semicircle, where a Presbyterian and myself shall be like Castor and Pollux, the one up and the other down; which, methinks, is like the worshipping the sun, and making him the deity, that we may be religious half the year, and every night serve another interest. Sir, the stipend is so inconsiderable, it will not pay the charge and trouble of removing myself and family. It is wholly arbitrary; for the triers may overthrow it; or the vicar may forbid it; or the subscribers may die, or grow weary, or poor, or be absent. I beseech you, sir, pay my thanks to your friend, who had so much kindness for me as to intend my benefit: I think myself no less obliged to him and you than if I had accepted it."

We add the conclusion of this letter, though fragmentary, for its sound counsel to his friend concerning his spiritual and temporal interests. It may appear at first sight that these are incongruously joined, but we are to remember the harassing effect of pecuniary difficulties upon the mind, and the great evils inflicted upon others by carelessness or irregularity in the discharge of obligations. Dr. Taylor had for many years felt in his own experience the weight of these cares.

"Sir," he continues, "I am well pleased with the pious meditations and the extracts of a religious spirit which I read in your excellent letter. I can say nothing at present but this: that I hope in a short progression you will be wholly immerged in the delices and joys of religion; and as I perceive your relish and gust of the things of the world goes off continually, so you will be invested with new capacities, and entertained with new appetites; I say with new appetites, for in religion every new degree of love is a new appetite; as in the schools we say, every single angel does make a species, and differs more than numerically from an angel of the same order.

"Your question concerning interest hath in it no difficulty as you have prudently stated it. For in the case, you have only made yourself a merchant with them; only you take less, that you be secured; as you pay a fine to the Assurance Office. I am only to add this. You are neither directly nor collaterally to engage the debtor to pay more than is allowed by law. It is necessary that you employ your money some way for the advantage of your family. You may lawfully buy land, or traffic, or exchange it to your profit. You may do this by yourself or by another, and you may as well get something as he get more, and that as well by money, as by land or goods; for one is as valuable in the estimation of merchants and of all the world as any thing else can be: and, methinks, no man should deny money to be valuable, that remembers every man parts with what he hath for money; and as lands are of a price when they are sold forever, and when they are parted with for a year, so is money; since the employment of it is as apt to minister to gain as lands are to rent. Money and lands are equally the matter of increase; to both of them our industry must be applied, or else the profit will cease: now as a tenant of lands may plough for me, so a tenant of money may go to sea and traffic for me."

It is not certain whether Dr. Taylor's objections were overcome and he accepted this lectureship, or that a new proposal was made. In either case the additional inducement was offered of a permanent provision for his family. Dr., afterwards Sir William Petty, who had recently made a survey of the island by order of the government, and had thus become intimately acquainted with the value of the forfeited estates, offered to purchase lands of this description for him at very low rates. This, added to introductions to persons of high authority, and the continued solicitations of Lord Conway, who promised him "many intimate kindnesses," led him to accept. Lord Conway was influenced not only by regard for Dr. Taylor, but by a laudable desire to improve the people who occupied his estates. "I thank God," he earnestly expresses himself to a relative, Major Rawdon, "I went upon a principle not to be repented of, for I had no interest or passion in what I did for him, but rather some reluctancy. What I pursued was, to do an act of piety towards all such as are truly disposed to virtue in those parts, for I am certain he is the choicest person in England appertaining to the conscience."

Dr. Taylor's decision was soon made, for in June we find him leaving London, provided with the promised introductions and a pass signed and sealed by the Lord Protector, for Antrim county, Ireland. His residence is supposed to have been near that of Lord Conway at Portmore. From this place he visited Lisburn, eight miles distant, now an important town, but then only a small village, as the duties of his lectureship called him. The mansion of Portmore, built not many years previously, after the designs of the celebrated architect Inigo Jones, in a style of great extent and splendor, stood in a beautiful park adorned by the waters of Lough Neagh, and the smaller Lough Bag, or Little Lake. It is a tradition of the neighborhood that the great divine often visited several of the beautiful little islands which adorn both of these sheets of water. Ram Island, which contains the ruins of a monastery and one of the round towers peculiar to the country, and which add much to the picturesqueness of many of its celebrated localities, is said to have been one of his especial favorites. Another was a smaller nook in the smaller lake. Both were within a mile from Portmore, and therefore at a convenient distance. A visitor some score of years since to the Lough, found upon one of its small islands the remains of a summer-house, in which Dr. Taylor is said to have frequently composed.*

In this pleasant retreat Dr. Taylor complet-

* Willmott's *Life of Jeremy Taylor*, p. 182.

ed his great work on *Cases of Conscience.* "I have kept close all the winter," he writes to Mr. Evelyn, "that I might without interruption attend to the finishing of the employment I was engaged in." His retirement and occupation are far from lessening his interest in the literary movement of the time. "Sir," he continues, "I pray, say to me something concerning the state of learning; how is any art and science likely to improve? what good books are lately public? what learned men, abroad or at home, begin anew to fill the mouth of fame, in the place of the dead Salmasius, Vossius, Mocelin, Sirmond, Rigaltius, Descartes, Galileo, Peiresk, Petavius, and the excellent persons of yesterday?"

This, like all his other letters from this place, breathes an air of contentment. He fully appreciated the natural beauties of this, as of his former retreat, addressing a friend, *ex amœnissimo recessu*, from my most pleasant recess, in Portmore. He was not entirely free from annoyance, a petty fellow, named Tandy, an agent of various large estates in the neighborhood, having denounced him to the Irish Privy Council as disaffected. An allusion to the affair occurs in a letter to Evelyn, dated, June

4, 1659. "I fear my peace in Ireland is likely to be short; for a Presbyterian and a madman have informed against me as a dangerous man to their religion; and for using the sign of the cross in baptism." In consequence of this charge Dr. Taylor was summoned to appear before the Irish Privy Council during the winter. His friend, Lord Conway, was much annoyed at Tandy's conduct. He took the matter up as his own personal affair, writing to a friend, "I hope, therefore, when you come over you will take him, Tandy, off from persecuting me, since none know better than yourself whether I deserve the same at his hands." "The quarrel is, it seems, because he thinks Dr. Taylor more welcome to Hillsborough than himself." The nobleman's influence, combined with that of others, was, probably, sufficient to procure Dr. Taylor's immediate discharge. His journey at an inclement season, had also brought on a severe illness, furnishing, as Bishop Heber suggests, an additional inducement for lenity.

It appears from another portion of this letter that Mr. Evelyn's bounty was still continued: "Sir, I do account myself extremely obliged to your kindness and charity, in your continued care of me and bounty to me; it is so much the more, because I have almost from all men but yourself, suffered some diminution of their kindness, by reason of my absence, for, as the Spaniard says, 'The dead and the absent have but few friends.' But, sir, I account myself infinitely obliged to you, much for your pension, but exceedingly much more for your affection, which you have so signally expressed. I pray, sir, be pleased to present my humble service to your two honoured brothers: I shall be ashamed to make any address, or pay my thanks in words to them, till my *Rule of Conscience* be public, and that is all the way I have to pay my debts; that and my prayers that God would.

* * * * * *

"Sir, I fear I have tired you with an impertinent letter, but I have felt your charity to be so great as to do much more than to pardon the excess of my affections. Sir, I hope that you and I remember one another when we are upon our knees."

Another letter to Mr. Evelyn, written not long after the death of Cromwell, presents a beautiful picture of devotion and friendship. "I long, sir, to come to converse with you;

for I promise to myself that I may receive from you an excellent account of your progression in religion, and that you are entered unto the experimental and secret way of it, which is that state of excellency whither good persons use to arrive after a state of repentance and caution. My retirement in this solitary place hath been I hope of some advantage to me as to this state of religion, in which I am yet but a novice, but by the goodness of God, I see fine things before me whither I am contending. It is a great, but a good work, and I beg of you to assist me with your prayers, and to obtain of God for me that I may arrive to that height of love and union with God, which is given to all those souls who are very dear to God.

CHAPTER XII.

THE DUCTOR DUBITANTIUM—DEATH OF CROMWELL—THE DECLARATION—DEDICATION—WORKS ON CASUISTRY—CONSCIENCE—ANCIENT CABINET—FRIAR CLEMENT—THE JEWISH LAW—SANCTITY OF CHURCHES—JUSTICE AND PIETY—RANDOM SHOTS—SCRUPLES—LIMITED OBLIGATIONS.

IN the following spring of 1660, Dr. Taylor visited London to superintend the publication of his *Ductor Dubitantium*. It was a fortunate journey for him, although from his allusion to public affairs in the letter just quoted from, he had evidently no expectation of the near triumph of the royalist party. He says, Nov. 3, 1659, "I must needs beg the favor of you that I may receive from you an account of your health and present conditions, and of your family; for I fear concerning all my friends, but especially for those few very choice ones I have, lest the present troubles may have done them any violence in their affairs or content. It is now long since that cloud passed; and though I suppose the sky is yet full of meteors and evil prognostics, yet you all have time to consider concerning your peace and your securities. That was not God's time to relieve his Church, and I cannot understand from what quarter that wind blew, and whether it was for us or against us. But God disposes all things wisely; and religion can receive no detriment or diminution but by our own fault." The allusion is of course to the death of the Lord Protector, Cromwell, in September, 1659. Richard Cromwell had, in the mean time, abdicated; the supreme power passed to the army, whose leaders had been induced by their associate, General Monk, to declare for Charles the Second.

Shortly before the landing of the king, a number of the leading members of the royalist party united in a "Declaration," designed to allay apprehension and promote quiet. As Dr. Taylor's name appears among those of its signers, we quote a portion as an expression of his views respecting this great political change. After thanking General Monk for his services, the paper continues as follows: "And because the enemies of the public peace have endeavored to represent those of the king's party, as men implacable, and such as would sacrifice the common good to their own private passions, we do sincerely profess, that we do reflect upon our past sufferings from the hands of God, and, therefore, do not cherish any violent thoughts or inclinations, to have been any way instrumental in them. And if the indiscretion of any spirited* persons transport them to expressions contrary to this our sense, we utterly disclaim them; and desire that the imputation may extend no further than the folly of the offenders. And we further declare, that we intend, by our quiet and peaceable behavior, to testify our submission to the present power, as it now resides in the Council of State, in expectation of the future Parliament, upon whose wisdom and determinations, we trust God will give such a blessing, as may produce a perfect settlement both in Church and State."

Dr. Taylor had soon after the gratification of dedicating the elaborate work, which he regarded as his masterpiece, to the monarch to whose cause he had so faithfully adhered. The *Ductor Dubitantium* appeared in June, 1660.

---

* A curious use of the word as the equivalent of *hasty, inconsiderate.*

This is by far the longest of Dr. Taylor's works. It is the one, as we have seen by frequent references in his letters, on which he was probably most willing his reputation should rest.

Under the old Roman Catholic system of the confessional, it became necessary to establish certain rules of guidance, for counsel and reproof, for those into whose ears the varied story of human doubt and frailty was constantly poured, and the most celebrated writers of the middle ages produced huge folios to supply this want. Casuistry became in their able hands a science. This necessity does not exist in our Protestant Church, and works of this kind must, therefore, possess a less practical value than they hold under a system which establishes a penitential or pecuniary tariff for sins. Every man's conscience must, to a very great extent, be left to establish its own rule. The "mind diseased," Shakespeare tells us, "must minister to itself." Although we can accept no uninspired book as an authoritative guide to a doubting conscience, we must be careful not to undervalue the aid which may be afforded by judicious advice. Our Church, though she has wisely banished the confessional, invites those who cannot quiet their consciences, to "come to the minister of God's word and open their grief." It is in the spirit of this invitation that Dr. Taylor has written. His work opens with a consideration of Conscience and the difficulties into which its errors, its debates, its doubts, and scruples lead it. He then passes to the Law of Nature, which he exhibits in its general applications, and as "commanded, digested, and perfected by our Supreme Lawgiver, Jesus Christ." Human laws are next discussed in their relations to the Church, the State, and the family. The fourth and last book treats of the nature and causes of good and evil.

It is plainly beyond our present limits to enter into any analysis of this remarkable work, It is, for the most part, closely argued, affording fewer passages than in Dr. Taylor's other writings of eloquent amplification. Many of his counsels on the details of every-day action are shrewd and practical, but many other doubtful points seem raised by the ingenuity of the student of books, rather than of men. The work overflows with curious learning. Authors of all ages and ranks are cited, and illustrations, often of a very strange character, introduced to enforce the writer's positions.

Bishop Heber concludes a long and careful examination of the *Ductor Dubitantium*, with a comparison most happily illustrating the peculiarities to which we have alluded. "It resembles," he says, "in some degree, those ancient inlaid cabinets (such as Evelyn, Boyle, or Wilkins, might have bequeathed to their descendants), whose multifarious contents perplex our choice, and offer, to the imagination or curiosity of a more accurate age, a vast wilderness of trifles and varieties, with no arrangement at all, or an arrangement on obsolete principles; but whose ebony drawers and perfumed recesses contain specimens of every thing that is precious, or uncommon, and many things for which a modern museum might be searched in vain."

We cannot better convey an idea to our readers of these peculiarities, than by opening a few of these "ebony drawers and perfumed recesses." Our extracts will serve our biographical purpose, by exhibiting the peculiarities of the author's mind quite as faithfully, perhaps, as some of his more elaborate passages.

FRIAR CLEMENT AND POOR DEMOISELLE FAUCETTE.

Friar Clement, the Jacobin, thinks, erroneously, that it is lawful to kill his king; the poor Demoiselle Faucette thinks it unlawful to spit in the church: but it happened that, one day, she did it against her conscience; and the Friar, with his conscience and a long knife, killed the king. If the question be here,—who sinned most? the disparity is next to infinite; and the poor woman was to be chidden for doing against her conscience, and the other to be hanged for doing according to his.

Book I, Chap. III, Rule IV.

THE JEWISH LAW.

The law that was wholly ceremonial and circumstantial, must needs pass away; and when they have lost their priesthood, they cannot retain the law; as no man takes care to have his beard shaved, when his head is off.

Book I, Chap. IV, Rule II.

SANCTITY OF CHURCHES.

Some think churches not to be more sacred than other places: what degree of probability soever this can have, yet it is a huge degree of folly to act this opinion, and to choose a barn to pray in, when a church may be had.

Book I, Chap. IV, Rule III.

JUSTICE AND PIETY.

Justice is like a knife, and hath a back and an edge, and there is a letter and a spirit in all laws, and justice itself is to be conducted with piety. * * * * *

As prudence sometimes must be called to counsel in the conduct of piety, so must piety oftentimes lead in justice; and justice itself must be sanctified by the word of God and prayer, and will then go on towards heaven, when both robes, like paranymphs * attending a virgin in the solemnities of her marriage, helped to lead and to adorn her.

Book I, Chap. IV, Rule X.

RANDOM SHOTS, AND QUESTIONABLE COUNSELS.

A Castilian gentleman, being new recovered from the sad effects of a melancholy spirit and an affrighting conscience, and being entertained by some that waited on him with sports and innocent pastimes, to divert his scaring thoughts, he with his company, shot

---

* Bridemaids.

many arrows in a public field, at rovers; at that time there was a man killed, whether by his arrows or no, he knew not, and is forbidden to inquire; and his case had in it reason enough to warrant the advice. The knowledge could not have done him so much good, as it would have done him hurt; and it was better he should be permitted to a doubting than to a despairing conscience, as in his case it was too likely to have happened. It is better to be suspected than to be seen.

* * * * * *

A priest, going to the West-Indies, by misfortune wounds one of his company, whom, with much trouble and sorrow, he leaves to be cured of his hurt, but passes on to his voyage, which he finished at a huge distance from the place of his misfortune. The merchants come the next year that way, and he is unwilling to inquire concerning his sick friend; desirous he was to know good of him, but infinitely fearful lest he be dead: consulting, therefore, with his superior in the case, was directed not to inquire, upon this account; because, if the man were dead, the priest would be irregular, and a whole parish unprovided for, and left without rites and sacraments and public offices, which then and there could not easily be supplied. Book I, Chap. V, Rule IV.

SCRUPLES.

Some scruple at an innocent ceremony, and against all conviction, and armies of reason, will be troubled and will not understand; this is very bad;—but it is worse that he should think himself the more godly man for being thus troubled and diseased, and that, upon this account, he shall fall out with government, and despise it; this man nurses his scruple till it proves his death; and instead of curing a boil, dies with a cancer: and is like a man that hath strained his foot, and keeps his bed for ease, but by lying there long, falls into a lipothymy,* and that bears him to his grave.

Book I, Chap. VI, Rule V.

LIMITED OBLIGATIONS.

Every man is bound to restore his neighbor's goods when they are demanded; but if he calls for his sword to kill a man withal,—there is equity in this case, and I am not guilty of the breach of the natural law, if I refuse to deliver him the sword, when he is so violent and passionate. Book II, Chap. I, Rule XII.

* A swoon.

CHAPTER XIII.

VACANT BISHOPRICS—DR. TAYLOR'S CLAIMS—APPOINTED TO DOWN AND CONNOR—MARQUIS OF ORMOND—THE WORTHY COMMUNICANT—VARIETY OF VIEWS—THE DOVE—CONSECRATION—BEREAVEMENT—INCUMBENTS OF PARISHES—AGREEMENT AT BREDA—CONFERENCE—SECTARIAN STRIFE IN BISHOP TAYLOR'S DIOCESE—SCOTCH AND IRISH—TRINITY COLLEGE—DROMORE—CONCILIATION.

DURING the long period of the suppression of Episcopacy many bishoprics had become vacant. These were now to be filled. On political grounds no one had better claim to promotion than Dr. Taylor. In those qualifications which rise far above all political grounds no one ever possessed greater claims. His piety and learning were admitted by his opponents as unreservedly as by his friends, and this too in an age in which the bitterness of sectarian hate was added to that apparently inseparable from political strife. He had borne adversity cheerfully, and in the pell mell of confiscations, losses and uncertainties, maintained by his industry an unblemished pecuniary reputation. He might have claimed, and, had he urged his claim, probably received, a far more important diocese than that of Down and Connor, in Ireland, to which he was speedily appointed. Dr. Taylor's wishes were however doubtless consulted. He had become attached to the district where he was now resident; forming a portion of the diocese over which he was called to preside. He was acquainted with its spiritual wants, and he was also perhaps loath to disturb his family, now comfortably established after many changes and privations. He was also, it is probable, strongly urged to accept the appointment by the Marquis, afterwards Duke of Ormond, a leading Irish nobleman and statesman, deeply interested in the welfare of the Irish Church, and desirous that her vacant bishoprics should be filled by earnest, vigorous, and talented men. Soon after his compliance, he was elected, by this gentleman's influence, vice-chancellor of the University of Dublin.

Before leaving England the Bishop-elect published "*The Worthy Communicant;* or, a Discourse of the Nature, Effect, and Blessings, consequent to the worthy receiving of the Lord's Supper, and of all the duties required in order to a worthy preparation: together with the Cases of Conscience occurring in the duty of him that ministers, and of him that communicates." The work was dedicated to Mary, eldest daughter of Charles the First, and the widowed mother of William, prince of Orange, afterwards king of England.

This volume contains one of his beautiful similes. The passage has an additional claim to our regard from its evidence of his charitable consideration for the opinions of others. "Let no man," he says, "be less confident in his holy faith and persuasion concerning the greatest blessings and glorious effects which God designs to every faithful and obedient soul in the communication of these divine mysteries, by reason of any difference of judgment which is in the several schools of Christians concerning the effects and consequent blessings of this sacrament. For all men speak honorable things of it, except wicked persons and the scorners of religion; and, though of several persons, like the beholders of a dove walking in the sun, as they stand in several aspects and distances, some see red, and others purple, and yet some perceive nothing but green, but all allow and love the beauties: so do the several forms of Christians, according as they are instructed by their first teachers, or their own experience, conducted by their fancy and proper principles, look upon these glorious mysteries." The volume also contained a sermon preached by Dr. Taylor at the funeral of Sir George Dalstone, of Dalstone, in Cumberland, September 28, 1657.

Dr. Taylor was consecrated bishop, with the other divines appointed to the vacant Irish dioceses, twelve in number, by the Archbishop of Dublin, Primate of Ireland, in St. Patrick's Cathedral, on the 27th of January, 1661. The sermon, from the forty-third verse of the twelfth chapter of St. Luke, was preached by Dr. Taylor, and afterwards included in the fifth edition of his discourses. In February following, he was appointed a member of the Irish Privy Council.

The joy of the family circle at the return of their beloved head invested with the high office of a bishop, at the reflection that his and their sharp pecuniary trials were now over, and home and competence secured, was saddened by a heavy grief. The oft-bereaved father was again called to mourn. His eldest and last remaining son was buried in the parish church at Lisburn, on the tenth of March, 1661.

The settlement of religious affairs in the United Kingdom was a task attended with much difficulty. Many Presbyterian and Independent clergymen had been placed in vacant benefices and were not therefore liable, like many placed in similar positions by the forcible ejection of the rightful incumbents, to a just call to yield their places to the former and rightful owners. It would have been well had the plan been followed to which Charles to some extent pledged himself at Breda, in the bargaining which returned him to the throne. By this agreement the first-mentioned class of ministers would have been left in peaceful possession of their benefices, with the understanding that they were to be succeeded after their decease by clergymen of the Church of England. Bishop Heber urges that dissent, deprived of cause of complaint, would have gradually yielded to the strongly expressed preference of the people for the Liturgy.

A different course was however naturally, though we cannot but think unhappily, adopted, whereby the use of the Prayer-Book was again uniformly imposed. An attempt was made by a conference to render this precious volume the bond of union of all English Protestants, but in spite of the exertions of Richard Baxter and Philip Henry, names to be ever held in reverence for learning and piety, moderation and charity, the plan was defeated. Churchmen did not yet appreciate the advantages of union. Dissenters, while admitting the pure doctrine and beauty of the Liturgy, and in many cases willing to submit to Episcopal government, maintained their old stand against wearing surplices, using the cross in Baptism, and kneeling at the Holy Communion.

Sectarian difference, more rife in Ireland than England, was nowhere more bitter than in the diocese of Bishop Taylor. The energetic suppression of the rebellion in Ireland by Cromwell had placed the island entirely in the power of his party. Church of England clergymen were superseded by Presbyterian or Independent preachers. The confiscated estates fell into the hands of individuals of the same religious persuasion, and the dissenting interest was further strengthened by the settlement of many Scotch in the northern part of the country.

The lower classes still adhered blindly to

their ancient faith, attached to it by hereditary custom and a feeling of nationality which endeared their belief from a fancied connection with the soil, and identified Protestantism with invasion and tyranny. There seems to be little doubt that the evil was, in a great degree, owing to the neglect of the English in not providing a clergy skilled in the native dialects of the island. Had this course been adopted at the opening of the English Reformation much subsequent difficulty might have been avoided.

The affairs of the university partook of the general embarrassment. Trinity College, Dublin, is familiar to us in this country from the initials T. C. D., which we have so often met appended to the names of our classical instructors in school and college. The buildings still occupy the vast green, in the heart of Dublin, granted, with large productive endowments, by Queen Elizabeth, the founder. During the Commonwealth the affairs of the college had become disordered. The revenues were impaired, a portion of the endowments alienated, and students and fellows admitted without regard to the requirements of the statutes. Bishop Taylor at once set himself to the labor, not only of restoring affairs to their former condition, but to completing the collection, arrangement, and revision of the college laws commenced by Bishop Bedell. He succeeded so well, that Bishop Heber attributes the high rank the institution has since maintained to the good order and discipline thus introduced.

In the April following Bishop Taylor's consecration, the small diocese of Dromore, adjoining his episcopal charge, was also placed under his care, "on account," in the words of the official record of his appointment, "of his virtue, wisdom, and industry."

The Bishop had need of these qualities. The general difficulties to which we have alluded, pressed nowhere with greater weight than in his dioceses. Many of the sternest Presbyterians had emigrated from the west of Scotland across the narrow waters to this inviting region. They retained all their attachment to the Covenant and dislike of Episcopacy. Their preachers formed a league among themselves "to speak with no bishops, and to endure neither their government nor their persons." They exhorted their congregations to pursue a similar course, denouncing alike the Episcopal office and its incumbent.

Bishop Taylor, meanwhile, pursued the conciliatory course reasonably to be expected from him by those familiar with his career. He labored earnestly in his vocation, preaching every Sunday in different churches, visiting his clergy, among whom the malcontents were included, inviting them to friendly conference on points of difference, and exerting himself to induce influential laymen to lend their aid in appeasing clerical strife. The clergy held aloof, but the laity were won by this fair and liberal course, so that by degrees the representatives of the principal estates and interests of the district came over, with one exception, to the Bishop's side, and it is asserted by Carte, in his life of the Duke of Ormond, that before the Act of Uniformity was passed, two years later, the majority of the clergy had been brought to a kindly appreciation of the Bishop's liberality.

CHAPTER XIV.

SERMON BEFORE THE IRISH PARLIAMENT—SURPLICES—JUSTICE—PITY—MR. EVELYN—CHOIR OF DROMORE CATHEDRAL—DR. RUST—SERMON BEFORE TRINITY COLLEGE—THE WOLF AT SCHOOL—REFORMATION—CONFIRMATION—SERMON AT THE FUNERAL OF THE LORD PRIMATE—THE HOPES OF MAN—THE TRIUMPH OF THE CROSS.

A PUBLIC occasion soon presented an opportunity for a full exhibition of the new Bishop's views. We find him, in his sermon delivered before both houses of the Irish Parliament, while alluding with, as we must consider, deserved censure to those who refused to wear a surplice, as "such as thought it a less sin to stand in separation from the Church, than to stand in a clean white garment," recommending to the fullest extent a course of conciliation on the one hand, and of abstinence from factious opposition on the other.

He pursues the same plan in reference to subjects of a social and political nature. He thus charges the legislators, by whom the questions respecting the confiscated estates were to be determined, a matter in which the property, feelings, and prejudices of almost the entire community were involved:

"Whatever you do, let not the pretence of a different religion make you think it lawful to oppress any man in his just rights; for opinions are not, but laws only, and 'doing as we would be done to,' are the measures of justice: and though justice does alike to all men, Jew and Christian, Lutheran and Calvinist, yet, to do right to them that are of another opinion is the way to win them; but if you, for conscience' sake, do them wrong, they will hate both you and your religion."

He enforces his reasoning, after his wonted manner by a beautiful simile :

MERCY.

Surely no man is so much pleased with his own innocence, as that he will be willing to quit his claim to mercy, and, if we all need it, let us all show it.

> Naturæ imperio gemimus, cum funus adultæ
> Virginis occurrit, vel terra clauditur infans,
> Et minor igne rogi!

If you do but see a maiden carried to her grave a little before her intended marriage, or an infant die before the birth of reason, nature has taught us to pay a tributary tear. Alas! your eyes will behold the ruin of many families, which, though they sadly have deserved, yet mercy is not delighted with the spectacle; and therefore God places a watery cloud in the eye, that, when the light of heaven shines on it, it may produce a rainbow, to be a sacrament and a memorial that God and the sons of God do not love to see a man perish. God never rejoices in the death of him that dies, and we also esteem it indecent to have music at a funeral. And as religion teaches us to pity a condemned criminal, so mercy intercedes for the most benign interpretation of the laws. You must, indeed, be as just as the laws: and you must be as merciful as your religion: and you have no way to tie these together, but to follow the pattern in the mount; do as God does, who in judgment remembers mercy.

On the sixteenth of November of this year, Bishop Taylor addressed a letter from Dublin to his friend Evelyn, written with his usual warmth. It is the last which has been preserved, and is supposed to have been the last which passed between the parties.

The cessation is to be attributed, not to any falling off in friendship, but to the usual effect of distance, diversity of occupation, and the want of any exciting cause to call forth a letter. We therefore are to part here with one of the most attractive characters of our narrative. It is pleasant to remember that Mr. Evelyn lived several years later, passing through the Revolution of 1688, and maintaining through all changes of dynasty and party, an amiable and honorable demeanor, which rendered him a favorite with all classes and sects.

Many years after Bishop Taylor's death, we find an allusion to Mary Marsh as "the daughter of his worthy and pious friend, the late Bishop of Down and Connor."

In this same year, Bishop Taylor rebuilt the choir of his cathedral at Dromore at his own expense, his wife presenting at the same time a set of communion plate. He also strengthened the clerical force of his diocese by inviting over George Rust, a fellow of Christ's College, Cambridge, and appointing him, soon after his arrival, to the deanery of Connor. Dr. Rust preached his friend's funeral sermon and succeeded him in his bishopric.

Bishop Taylor's liberality was not confined

to church restoration. Dr. Rust's sermon bears emphatic testimony to the extent of his benefactions at this period. "He was not only a good man Godwards, but he was come to the top of St. Peter's gradation, and to all his other virtues added a large and diffusive charity; and whoever compares his plentiful incomes with the inconsiderable estate he left at his death, will be easily convinced that charity was steward for a great proportion of his revenue. But the hungry that he fed, and the naked that he clothed, and the distressed that he supplied, and the fatherless that he provided for; the poor children that he put to apprentice, and brought up at school, and maintained at the university, will now sound a trumpet to that charity which he dispersed with his right hand, but would not suffer his left hand to have any knowledge of it."

In 1662, Bishop Taylor printed his *Via Intelligentiæ*, a sermon preached before the University of Dublin. It follows the train of thought of his *Liberty of Prophesying*, showing us that holiness is the best protection against the reception or growth of error, and that the aid of the Holy Spirit will be extended to all who seek its guidance to truth. He qualifies the universal range of this sentiment by the declaration, that if "by opinions men rifle the affairs of kingdoms, it is also as certain, they ought not to be made public and permitted;" an admission of a dangerous character from the difficulty of restraining it within proper bounds.

We extract two characteristic passages from this discourse.

THE WOLF AT SCHOOL.

Every man understands by his affections, more than by his reason; and when the wolf in the fable went to school to learn to spell, whenever letters were told him, he could never make any thing of them but *agnus;* he thought of nothing but his belly: and if a man be very hungry, you must give him meat before you give him counsel.

REFORMATION.

We talk much of reformation; and (blessed be God) once we have felt the good of it: but of late we have smarted under the name and pretension: the woman that lost her groat, *everrit domum*, not *evertit:* she swept the house, she did not turn the house out of doors. That was but an ill reformation that untiled the roof, and broke the walls, and was digging down the foundations.

In the following year, Bishop Taylor added "A Defence and Introduction to the Rite of Confirmation," three Sermons preached at Dublin, and a Funeral Discourse on the Primate, Archbishop Bramhall, to the long list of his writings. The Funeral Discourse contains two of his finest passages.

THE HOPES OF MAN.

As a worm creeping with her belly on the ground, with her portion and share of Adam's curse, lifts up her head to partake a little of the blessings of the air, and opens the junctures of her imperfect body, and curls her little rings into knots and combinations, drawing up her tail to a neighborhood of the head's pleasure and motion; but still it must return to abide the fate of its own nature, and dwell and sleep upon the dust: so are the hopes of a mortal man; he opens his eyes and looks upon fine things at a distance, and shuts them again with weakness, because they are too glorious to behold; and the man rejoices because he hopes fine things are staying for him; but his heart aches because he knows there are a thousand ways to fail and miss of those glories; and though he hopes, yet he enjoys not; he longs, but he possesses not; and must be content with his portion of dust, and being *a worm and no man*, must lie down in this portion, before he can receive the end of his hopes, the salvation of his soul in the resurrection of the dead.

THE TRIUMPH OF THE CROSS.

Presently it came to pass, that men were no longer ashamed of the cross, but it was worn upon breasts, printed in the air, drawn upon foreheads, carried upon banners, put upon crowns imperial; presently it came to pass, that the religion of the despised Jesus did infinitely prevail: a religion that taught men to be meek and humble, apt to receive injuries, but unapt to do any; a religion that gave countenance to the poor and pitiful, in a time when riches were adored, and ambition and pleasure had possession of the heart of all mankind; a religion that would change the face of things, and the hearts of men, and break vile habits into gentleness and counsel; that such a religion, in such a time, by the sermons and conduct of fishermen, men of mean breeding and illiberal arts, should so speedily triumph over the philosophy of the world, and the arguments of the subtle, and the sermons of the eloquent; the power of princes and the interests of states, the inclinations of nature and the blindness of zeal, the force of custom and the solicitation of passions, the pleasures of sin and the busy arts of the devil; that is, against wit and power, superstition and wilfulness, fame and money, nature and empire, which are all the causes in this world that can make a thing impossible; this, this is to be ascribed to the power of God, and is the great demonstration of the resurrection of Jesus. Every thing was an argument for it, and improved it; no objection could hinder it, no enemies destroy it; whatsoever was for them, it made the religion to increase; whatsoever was against them, it made it to increase; sunshine and storms, fair weather or foul, it was all one as to the event of things: for they were instruments in the hands of God, who could make what himself should choose to be the product of any cause; so that if the Christians had peace, they went abroad and brought in converts; if they had no peace, but persecution, the converts came in to them. In prosperity they allured and enticed the world by the beauty of holiness; in affliction and trouble they amazed all men with the splendor of their innocence, and the glories of their patience; and quickly it was that the world became disciple to the glorious Nazarene, and men could no longer doubt of the resurrection of Jesus, when it became so demonstrated by the certainty of them that saw it, and the courage of them that died for it, and the multitudes of them that believed it; who by their sermons and their actions, by their public offices and discourses, by festivals and eucharists, by arguments of experience and sense, by reason and religion, by persuading rational men, and establishing believing Christians, by their living in the obedience of Jesus, and dying for the testimony of Jesus, have greatly advanced his kingdom, and his power, and his glory, into which he entered after his resurrection from the dead. For he is the first-fruits; and if we hope to rise through him, we must confess that himself is first risen from the dead.

CHAPTER XV.

DISSUASIVE FROM POPERY—OBSTACLES TO PROTESTANTISM IN IRELAND—IRISH CLERGY—DUEL—CHARLES TAYLOR—DEATH—POSTHUMOUS WORKS—DR. RUST'S SERMON—BISHOP TAYLOR'S REMAINS—HIS WIDOW AND DAUGHTERS—WILLIAM TODD JONES—EDWARD JONES—PERSONAL APPEARANCE—PORTRAITS.

IN 1664, Bishop Taylor published a *Dissuasive from Popery*, prepared at the request of his brother prelates. The reformed doctrines had as yet made but little impression upon the uneducated Irish people. The fault lay to a great extent with their English rulers, who in their desire to make the English language supplant the native dialect, and partly perhaps from sheer neglect, omitted to send preachers practised in the Irish language among the people. Instead of this, an establishment was set up, and the people required not only to support but to attend, under penalty of fine, a service which was unintelligible to them. They were not even supplied with a Bible which they could read.

Another difficulty lay in the differences among the Protestants. Many of these were Calvinists, and almost as bitterly opposed to the Church of England as to the Church of Rome. Concerted action seemed therefore impossible. Single individuals had from time to time attempted some proselytizing movements, and with marked success, but this had not encouraged to any wider effort.

The Roman Catholic clergy were meanwhile using every exertion to perpetuate their hold upon the people. One of the most efficient means to accomplish this was by identifying their religious belief with the feeling against English rule. So far as they could, and their power was, as it has continued, great, they kept their congregations in ignorance.

Bishop Taylor's treatise was not intended to meet the wants of the common people, except through the medium of instructors. He sets forth in it, the great arguments furnished by the learned and able heads of the Reformation against the corruptions of Rome. He has himself alluded to the obstacles in the way of reaching the ear of the many. "We humbly desire of God," he devoutly says, "to accept and to bless this well-meant labor of love, and that by some admirable ways of his providence, he will be pleased to convey to them, the notices of their danger and their sin, and to deobstruct the passages of necessary truth to them; for we know the arts of their guides, and that it will be very hard that the notice of these things shall ever be suffered to arrive to the common people, but that which hinders will hinder, until it be taken away; however, we believe and hope in God for remedy."

It is to be regretted, that, as Bishop Heber suggests, a remedy was not sought for this state of things by the education of missionaries to address the people in their own tongue. This, however, could not have been accomplished by Bishop Taylor without the co-operation of his brother bishops and the government, but it is to be regretted that he did not see and point out some plan of the kind.

This was the last of Bishop Taylor's publications, and when we speak of the end of his literary career, the reader will be prepared for the speedy close of all his earthly affairs; for his hand, so practised and industrious in authorship, was not one to drop the pen until the last moment. The little intervening space was, however, like almost all the years that had gone, marked by trouble. Bishop Taylor had, as we have seen, buried not long before the only remaining son of his second marriage. Two sons by the first union were left. One of these, a captain of horse in the king's service, engaged in a duel with a brother officer of the name of Vane, in which both were mortally wounded. It was a sore death to die, at once the perpetrator and the victim of violence, and however the then prevalent laws of society may have fallen short of the condemnation they would now pronounce, we cannot but believe that if the sad news reached his ear, the father's sorrow at his son's death, deepened into anguish over its unworthy cause. He must have thought sadly of his own words in "The Apples of Sodom," "If his children prove vicious or degenerous, cursed or unprosperous, we account the man miserable, and his grave to be strewed with sorrows and dishonors." After quoting in the same discourse from classic story, many examples of unworthy sons of noble sires, he concludes "posterity did weep afresh over the monuments of their brave progenitors, and found that infelicity can pursue a man and overtake him in his grave."

The second son, Charles, was designed for

Holy Orders. He was qualified for the degree of Master of Arts at Trinity College, Dublin, but instead of entering the Church, pursued the very opposite course of becoming the companion and at last the secretary of the profligate Duke of Buckingham, in whose house at Baynard's Castle he died of a decline, and was buried in St. Margaret's church, Westminster, on the second of August, 1667. It is surmised that the father may have been spared the knowledge of this second bereavement, as he was the day after the funeral stricken with a fever, which in the brief space of ten days reached a fatal termination on the thirteenth of August.

A second part of the *Dissuasive from Popery*, prepared in reply to certain strictures on the first part, by John Serjeant, a Romish priest, was in the hands of the printer at the time of the author's decease. It was soon after published. Another posthumous work, a *Discourse on Christian Consolation*, appeared in 1671, and *Contemplations on the State of Man*, a production apparently unfinished and unrevised, followed in 1684.

Bishop Taylor was buried in the church at Dromore. The funeral sermon was preached by his friend Dr. Rust, who succeeded to his vacant episcopate. The discourse is much in the style of the deceased Bishop's pulpit compositions. It contains a brief outline of his friend's career, and a most eulogistic enumeration of his virtues. "To sum up all in a few words," he says, "this great prelate had the good humor of a gentleman, the eloquence of an orator, the fancy of a poet, the acuteness of a schoolman, the profoundness of a philosopher, the wisdom of a counsellor, the sagacity of a prophet, the reason of an angel, and the piety of a saint; he had devotion enough for a cloister, learning enough for a university, and wit enough for a college of *virtuosi:* and had his parts and endowments been parcelled out among his poor clergy that he left behind him, it would, perhaps, have made one of the best dioceses in the world."

The Bishop's remains were deposited in a vault beneath the communion table. This vault was opened about the year 1826, and found to contain a leaden coffin, marked with the initials, J. T. His resting-place remained unmarked by any memorial until 1827, when Bishop Mant united with the clergy of his diocese in placing a white marble tablet in the interior of Lisburn Cathedral. The slab bears an appropriate inscription. It is decorated on the right side by a crosier, and at the top by a sarcophagus, on which rests a Bible and mitre.

Bishop Heber states that the remains were disturbed a century after the interment to give place for the coffin of a recently deceased prelate, and that they were afterwards reverently replaced by a worthy successor, Bishop Percy, the editor of the "Reliques."

Dr. Mant, in his *History of the Church of Ireland*, has well nigh disproved this story. He shows that but one bishop, Marlay, died in possession of the see of Dromore, from 1713 to the commencement of Bishop Percy's administration in 1781. Bishop Marlay died suddenly at Dublin in 1763. There is no evidence that the place of his interment was at Dromore, or, if it was, that the former tenant of the vault made way for the new.

Bishop Taylor's widow lived for several years after her husband's decease. Three daughters survived him. The eldest, Phœbe, died unmarried. Mary, the second, the wife of Dr. Francis Marsh, afterwards Bishop of Limerick, and Archbishop of Dublin, has numerous descendants. Joanna, the third, married Edward Harrison, for many years the representative of Lisburn, in the Irish Parliament. One of their descendants, William Todd Jones, also the representative of Lisburn, collected materials from the family papers for the Bishop's biography. Among these were, Bishop Heber informs us, "a series of autograph letters to and from the Bishop; and a 'family book' also in his own handwriting, giving an account of his parentage, and the principal events of his life, with comments on many of the public transactions in which he himself, or those connected with him, had borne a share." Mr. Jones was prevented, by his sudden death in 1818, from accomplishing his design, and his papers have unfortunately disappeared. His brother, Edward Jones, is reported by Bishop Heber, as "solicitor-general to the State of North Carolina, where he is now living, with a numerous family."

Bishop Taylor seems to have retained through life much of the personal beauty which was so often noticed on his first appearance as a preacher. His portrait was frequently engraved during his life for various editions of his writings. He appears to have twice sat to artists. The first-executed painting is known only by a copy, the original having been lost in a river during the removal of the owner's effects. It presents a pleasing, cheerful countenance, with an aquiline nose, full, dark, benevolent eyes, and curling hair. The second portrait, in the Hall of All Souls' College, Oxford, was taken at a later period. The full eye and benevolent expression remain, but a grave air is spread over the features and a closer cap has taken the place of the flowing locks. We have copied an engraving from the first of these in the illustration to this volume. An excellent engraving of the second is prefixed to Bishop Heber's edition of his works.

CHAPTER XVI.

THE SHAKESPEARE OF THEOLOGY—BOOKS AND NATURE—A LIBRARY OF THEOLOGY—EXTRACTS—AMPLIFICATION—VARIED LEARNING—AN INDUSTRIOUS AND PRACTISED WRITER—NOT AN ASCETIC—DEDICATIONS—ELOQUENCE—ORIGINAL DELIVERY—PERMANENCE OF REPUTATION—PARALLEL—CONCLUSION.

JEREMY TAYLOR has been called the Shakespeare of Theology. The title was conferred by one of the first critics and philosophers of English literature, Samuel Taylor Coleridge, and its truth and beauty have been so widely recognized that it now seems inseparable from the name. Taylor was a far greater scholar than Shakespeare, but he used books as the poet used nature, culling everywhere some form of beauty. Many of his finest allusions, his most eloquently told and aptly pointed narratives, are from old forgotten folios of scholastic lore, requiring an insight, patience, and charity to educe living thought and practical good akin to that which found

> "Sermons in stones, books in the running brooks,
> And good in every thing."

But the great scholar of books was far from forgetting nature. His soul was too full of the love of God to neglect the manifestations of His goodness in "all things both great and small." He has drawn illustrations constantly from natural objects: the music of birds, the swaying of the tree-tops, the beauty of flowers, the glory of blended earth and sky, are all reproduced in his pages. A dweller for the greater part of his life among rural scenes, it is evident that he enjoyed and assimilated their beauties.

Bishop Taylor resembles Shakespeare in the wide spread of his sympathies, and the wide range of his thought. He has furnished us in his writings with almost a complete library of theology. He has guided our public and private devotions, has preached to us, has told us the story of our Saviour's life, has prepared us for the sacraments and rites of the Church, has given us instruction for our conduct in life and preparation for death, has defended the doctrines of the Church from the attacks of Romanist and dissenter, and furnished a "Rule of Conscience," for the regulation of our public and private acts.

Bishop Taylor delights in amplification. He builds up a simile or an argument, adding sentence to sentence, running on sometimes for a page or two without resting at a period, so that we have some difficulty in returning to the main subject of the discourse. This conveys an impression of diffuseness, when the fault does not really exist, for we shall find this extraneous matter as full of thought and conscientious labor as the rest. The long sentences at first seem involved, but if we examine them carefully, we shall find their construction simple.

The learning of Jeremy Taylor, was, as we have seen, of the most extended and varied nature. He has not only the Fathers and the Councils but the Jewish rabbis and the Eastern philosophers at his fingers' ends. He is at home not only with the classical authors of Greece and Rome, but with obscure writers of the two Empires. He draws so many illustrations from medical science, that if inclined to the theoretical style of biography we might allege that he had been a student at his brother-in-law's apothecary shop. He is familiar with the science of his day, the entire range of history, and an allusion to the "Grand Cyrus" shows that the fashionable novel of the time was not beneath his notice. This mass of erudition, which would be remarkable in any long life of learned leisure, becomes a still greater marvel when we remember Dr. Taylor's unsettled career, and the limited opportunities he must have enjoyed, even in his retirement at Golden Grove, and in Ireland, for consulting great collections of books.

The vast bulk of Bishop Taylor's writings bear evidence, with his store of learning, not only to wonderful industry and memory, but to wonderful powers of rapid literary composition. Some of his most elaborate productions were prepared in the hubbub of the camp, or the school-house. Others were written when a strong effort of will must have been needed, as he sat down to his desk, to drive away for a time the anxieties of the prison, the hiding-place, the wife and children in poverty. He must at times have written hastily as well as rapidly, and to this may be attributed his occasional error in citing, for chance illustration, evident fable for veritable history, some trick of alchemy as scientific truth; or yielding a too easy credence to the gorgon tales of some far wandering traveller.

Jeremy Taylor has been called an ascetic. To "youth and joy," the solemn subject and style of his volumes are probably not attractive, but we have not far to travel over the rough path of the world, to give us cause to turn with thankfulness to their warning and consolation. They must be judged from the fair ground of an average experience. His style maintains a fitting gravity and elevation, but we look in vain for any sympathy with the repressive system of the monk, the Puritan, or the dyspeptic school of modern times, which would turn the wedding-wine back to water, stop the music and dancing which gladdened the ear of the returning prodigal, and substitute "a dinner of herbs" for the fatted calf of the domestic board. Dr. Taylor's writings, far from showing a lack of sympathy with the innocent enjoyments of health and vigor, or the merciful alleviations of pain and sickness, exhibit their writer as one who had a hearty sympathy with home, and family, and the world at large. The whole tenor of his life bears a like genial testimony. He was so far from undervaluing cheerfulness, that he has, in several of his illustrations, given evidence both of the possession and appreciation of humor.

The dedications which Bishop Taylor prefixed to his different works are long and profuse in compliment. A charge has been based upon them, that their author was a mean flatterer of the great. It seems to us a sufficient answer to this charge, that one of these dedications was addressed to a king virtually dethroned, and kept its place after the monarch's head had fallen from the block. Another is also found in the formal custom of the time. An introduction to the translation of the Bible addressed to Queen Victoria, would not probably be written in the style of that addressed to Jame sthe First; and Jeremy Taylor, if writing at the present day, would probably word his dedications in a more condensed form than he adopted two hundred years ago. The faults of the time must not be weighed too heavily on the shoulders of the individual.

It is as hard to describe the eloquence of Jeremy Taylor, as to portray the clouds piled on clouds, now all aglow with the ruddy glory of the sunset, now dark and terrible with presage of the coming tempest. He heaps illustration upon illustration, and blends sonorous phrase of trumpet tone with gentle words of lute-like whisper, in such profusion and at such length, that we sometimes pant in following him.

These sermons, suggestive of cathedral grandeur, which should seem to have been delivered before princes and potentates, before mighty armies girded for battle, before the vast city throng elated by public rejoicing, or bowed in a common grief at the open grave of some great benefactor, found their first auditors in quiet village churches. We fancy the great sentences bounding back upon the speaker from the narrow wall. We fancy him soon wearying of intellectual toil for such inconsiderable results. Why spread so magnificent a feast for so few guests? He remembered the liberality of the Church at whose altar he served. The sublimities of her Liturgy were lavished in all their fulness on the humble as on the mighty, on the gathered two or three as on the innumerable throng. The Church always gave her best, and he followed her example.

A simpler style might perhaps have been better adapted to an uneducated auditory, but it is by no means probable that Jeremy Taylor's small congregations were entirely made up of unlearned men. The troubles of the times drove many of high birth and culture to retirement. Golden Grove was for some time near the scene of action, and many no doubt improved the opportunity of hearing the great divine. The ordinary household of Golden Grove was, as we have seen, graced by intellectual and moral worth, and constantly reinforced by guests of like disposition.

It matters little now, whether the auditors of Jeremy Taylor were few or many, rich or poor, whether they listened or dozed beneath his pulpit. The sound of his noble sermons went forth through the little chapel windows to the world beyond as effectually as if it had first hovered over a sea of faces, and echoed from pointed arch or rounded dome. It has gone forth to all lands, and is heard in well nigh every household.

His *Holy Living and Dying*, *The Great Exemplar*, the *Golden Grove*, and other devotional works have not only kept place with the *Sermons* in their fame, but have won a still more enviable place in the affection of those who care for such things. The *Holy Living and*

Dying has been the constant companion of the midway and closing years of many. *The Great Exemplar* has often passed, hallowed by pious hopes, from the trembling hand of age to the firm grasp of youth. The *Golden Grove* has brought a better than golden comfort to the humble closet and the sick man's pillow.

We can easily trace a parallel to the darker days of this great career. Jeremy Taylor, in his little country parish, struggling to support a wife and children by teaching school to eke out a scanty stipend, furnishes a picture to be readily matched in our own time and clime, but too often unrelieved by the genialities of a Golden Grove or the sympathies of a Countess of Carbery. We cannot hope that a commensurate success will follow a commensurate privation, that all young country parsons will turn out Jeremy Taylors, or even bishops. They may, however, follow out the suggestions connected with the surname rather than the baptismal appellation of our divine, and instead of lamenting that their lot is cast with the unappreciative, "whose talk is of bullocks," do their best cheerfully and unweariedly in a remote and limited sphere. The MS. volume of sermons may come back in the same brown paper travelling-dress in which it departed, instead of reappearing in the beauty of type, wafted over a sea of glory by favoring blasts from complimentary newspapers. The call may be long in coming, but the true scholar and clergyman will in some way find fit utterance, and be honored and prized by all to whom the Church, the Church of the struggling present as well as of the glorious past, is dear.

THE END.

From The Church Book Society, 762 Broadway, New York:—

The Lives of the Bishops:

LIFE OF BISHOP BASS,

LIFE OF BISHOP PROVOST,

LIFE OF BISHOP STEWART.

These are the three last of the excellent series in course of publication by the Episcopal Sunday School Union, and written by the Rev. J. N. Norton. They have more than usual interest; the first two embrace periods of history generally interesting to all. The life of Bishop Bass, of Massachusetts, gives us a picture of the early life of that far-famed colony, and biographical sketches of many prominent men, as well as the central portrait, its first bishop.

Bishop Provost, of New York, was consecrated at the close of the Revolutionary struggle, and his life necessarily attracts historical anecdotes and sketches of great value, many of them quite new.

Bishop Stewart, of Quebec, was a rare instance of self-denying earnestness, in the work of his Master. He was the son of the Earl of Galloway, but gave up rank and place for the life of a frontier missionary, living in the most absolute simplicity, and giving his large private income away in public and private charities. The story shames us who sit at ease and *wish* the world made better. —*Godey's Lady's Book.*

UNCA: A Story for Girls.

By the author of "Uncle Jack, the Fault-Killer."

Charmingly simple, and very attractive to children from six to ten. We recommend it for our Juvenile Library, No. 2.

MOTES IN THE SUNBEAM, and

THE CIRCLE OF BLESSING.

BY MRS. THOMAS GATTY.

As children's books have a double work to do—instructing the grown-up pupils of a family, as well as the children they are ostensibly provided for—we shall not quarrel with these fascinating little volumes because the moral of the tale and sometimes its arrangement are above the comprehension of young readers. Some knowledge of natural history and much experience of life are required before their lessons, or even the graceful and happily-turned allusions with which they abound, can be fully appreciated. We commend them to all mothers, both for "pleasure and profit."

In **OLD FRIENDS WITH NEW FACES,** by ALOE, we have those standard favorites: "Blue Beard," "The Genii and Fishermen," the "Singing Fountain," etc., paraphrased into most ingeniously instructive allegories. "Blue Beard," for instance, is "Baron Procrastination," and slays the charming brides, "Study-Well," "Work-Well," "Please-my-Mother," "Speak-Kindly," "Help-Others," and "Rise-Early;" while "Consider-Well," the last, is only rescued by Sister "Try's" help, who discovers the brothers "Firmness" and "Sense" coming to pay them a visit. We wish we were "a boy again," when we see such aids to "Good Resolution" held out to this rising generation.—*Godey's Lady's Book.*

We have learned to welcome the packages of the Protestant Episcopal Sunday School Union, assured that all their publications are useful, and many of them have rare merit. As a holiday gift suited to school-girls, we notice

ELLIE RANDOLPH,

By Miss Kitty J. Neely,

a volume approaching the single tales of Miss Yonge in size, and which has for its purpose the illustration of the truth that those who choose "the good part" with Mary, accomplish, by their quiet and consistent lives, more than Martha with her busy spirit and many cares. It is a story of Southern life, the characters well drawn, the aim of the book gradually unfolded, and the scenes touching or spirited, as the occasion demands. The whole tone of the book is admirable. Miss Neely is the sister of Mrs. Bradley, whose "Bread upon the Waters" and "Douglass Farm" are known to many of our readers.

CHRISTMAS VIGILS and **CHRISTMAS EARNINGS** are two excellent little stories for younger children.

With some of the **HYMNS FOR A CHRISTIAN CHILD,** our own little people have before this been made familiar. They are intended for quite young children.

"Little children must be quiet,
When to holy church they go,"

"The Christmas Hymn," and "Do no Sinful Action," are among their favorites.

LITTLE FOOTPRINTS is the suggestive title of a touching little story of the life and death of "a Christian child."—*Newspaper.*

Catechism of the Bible:

The Church teaches her children not only to read the Word of God, but to pray that they may also "mark, learn, and inwardly digest" that heavenly food of the soul. To follow out the figure presented in the last of these significant words, the *digesting*, it is necessary that the Holy Book be read, not only in large portions at a time, but be studied with a minute and particular care, without which its most nutritious parts are apt to escape the mind, and be thrown off as little better than chaff. To bring out this faithful thoroughness, there is no method like the old catechetical system—the Church system *par èminence*. Major E. D. Townsend has furnished the Church with a catechetical volume of over 300 pages, devoted to the elucidation of the *Pentateuch*. The questions and answers are brief and pertinent, the answers being for the most part embodied in the very words of Scripture, and from any part of it which best illustrates the subject in hand. The meanings of Hebrew names are given also, and many details of ancient manners and customs which render clearer the meaning of Holy Writ. Each *Lesson* is divided, moreover, into two parts, the former of which is suitable for younger children, and the latter for those that are further advanced. To the latter are appended *Remarks*, distinguished by brevity, good sense, and a devout and churchlike tone of thought and feeling, which give them no slight value. It is an unusual occurrence, and one well worthy of special mention, that it is the Senior Major in the United States Army who has thus carefully prepared a book like this for the instruction of the children of the Church.—*Church Journal.*

THE

LIFE OF GEORGE HERBERT

BY

GEORGE L. DUYCKINCK.

George Herbert is of all England's sacred poets the most sure of an enduring fame. He was a true poet. His life, too, was a very lovely one—that of a true Christian, of a scholar, a gentleman, and a faithful parish priest. More than this, he was beloved of dear old Izaak Walton, who wrote his life with that sweet homeliness of style which wins all honest hearts to him. Mr. Duyckinck has undertaken, in this pretty little volume, to set forth Herbert's life again "with a simplicity of style and fulness of detail which should in some degree meet the requirements both of youthful and mature readers." He has been very successful in a not very easy task. He has come to the work imbued with a love of his subject, and thoroughly understanding it; and he writes with an unaffected earnestness and purity quite in keeping with it. The young reader will find much valuable and interesting information in the book, upon matters kindred to or connected with its main purpose; and it is calculated to foster a correct literary taste, no less than to beget a healthy moral tone.—*Courier and Enquirer.*

BIOGRAPHY OF THE

REV. HENRY MARTYN.

BY THE REV. D. P. SANFORD, M.A.,

OF BROOKLYN.

With a Portrait and Illustrations.

This work is prepared in a very careful and interesting style. The peculiar warmth, strength, and depth of Martyn's personal experience, with all its sensitiveness, tenderness, and wonderful boldness and energy, are faithfully preserved, and illustrated with copious extracts from his private diary and correspondence. The more church-like features of his character, principles, and practice are not omitted or ignored, as is too commonly the case, but are fairly and truthfully stated. His extraordinary labors in the East—the breaking the soil, and watering the ground with his tears, and sowing the seed of the Word of Life—all this is narrated with genial spirit and patient minuteness, until his life of wondrous youth was crowned by an early death. Martyn, more than any other man, has been the germinant spirit of the missionary enterprise that now distinguishes the Church; and the vast power of his spiritual energy has made itself widely felt among the denominations around us, as well as among ourselves. His name has been music upon ten thousand tongues, and yet breathes fragrance from ten times ten thousand hearts. Mr. Sanford has done the Church a great service in placing so excellent a memoir of such a man on the shelves of our Sunday School libraries, where it will have the best chance to impregnate minds yet fresh and young with the best life of Martyn's singular self-devotion, and gentle, loving, and therefore irresistible, power.

THE BOY MISSIONARY.

BY MRS. JENNY MARSH PARKER.

The Boy Missionary is one of the best things the Church Book Society has given us in a long while. The idea is, to show how a poor little boy—weak, sickly, and not able to study much—may have the spirit of a missionary, and may, among his fellows, do the work of a missionary, too, even in boyhood; while others, of more brilliant parts and more commanding social position, look forward to missionary life as something future and far distant, and find their days brought to an end before their work is even begun. The authoress, Jenny Marsh Parker, shows no small knowledge of boy nature, and the temptations incident to the life of boys in a country village. Davie Hall will make many missionaries, both for the Far West and for home.—*Church Journal.*

The Life of George Herbert.

BY GEORGE L. DUYCKINCK.

New York, 1858: pp. 197.

WE have too long neglected to do our share in bringing this delightful little book to the notice of the lovers of holy George Herbert, among whom we may safely reckon a large number of the readers of the "Atlantic." It is based on the life by Izaak Walton, but contains much new matter, either out of Walton's reach or beyond the range of his sympathy.

Notices are given of Nicholas Ferrar and other friends of Herbert. There is a very agreeable sketch of Bemerton and its neighborhood, as it now is, and the neat illustrations are of the kind that really illustrate. The Brothers Duyckinck are well known for their unpretentious and valuable labors in the cause of good letters and American literary history, and this is precisely such a book as we should expect from the taste, scholarship, and purity of mind which distinguish both of them. It is much the best account of Herbert with which we are acquainted.—*Atlantic Monthly.*

www.ingramcontent.com/pod-product-compliance
Lightning Source LLC
LaVergne TN
LVHW011224110826
845150LV00006B/1532